CW01010968

Excel Version 5 for Windows Quick Reference

Que Quick Reference Series

Shelley O'Hara
Janice A. Snyder
Christopher Van Buren

Publisher
David P. Ewing

Director of Publishing
Michael Miller

Publishing Manager
Don Roche, Jr.

Managing Editor
Corinne Walls

Product Director
Joyce J. Nielsen

Development and Production Editor
Jill D. Bond

Technical Editor
Janice A. Snyder

Book Designer
Amy Peppler-Adams

Production Team
Paula Carroll, Scott Cook, Carla Hall, Michael Hughes,
Joy Dean Lee, Caroline Roop, Nanci Sears Perry,
Tina Trettin, Mary Beth Wakefield, Donna Winter

Table of Contents

Introduction

Welcome to *Excel Version 5 for Windows Quick Reference*. This book is designed as a handy guide and reference for both new and experienced users of Microsoft Excel Version 5 for Windows software. The book assumes a familiarity with Microsoft Windows, but does not assume that you have ever used Excel for Windows.

What is Excel for Windows?

Excel Version 5 for Windows is a full-featured spreadsheet program designed to run in Microsoft Windows. Excel Version 5 for Windows uses the graphical power of Windows to the utmost so that you can easily view and work with your data in an intuitive fashion, giving you visual access to your data.

Excel Version 5 for Windows is similar to other versions of Excel in its basic functions, and can be used for simple applications or complex financial planning. The program can organize data and includes typical database functions such as sorting, extracting, and finding data, as well as the capability to access external databases. With Excel Version 5 for Windows, you can produce graphic representations of financial and scientific data, and create macros that automate common worksheet tasks.

New Features

Excel Version 5 for Windows contains several new features, including a new workbook model, new worksheet features, pivot tables, data manipulation, and charting enhancements.

The new workbook model contains sheet tabs for quick access, 16 worksheets, and formatting properties for each worksheet. New worksheet features include the capability to audit your worksheet and new toolbars that enable you to customize your worksheet.

Excel Version 5 also provides ease-of use. The Chart Wizard walks you through creating charts for your worksheets. The Function Wizard shows you how to enter functions. The Tip Wizard gives you pointers on how to perform tasks more quickly.

Pivot tables, new with Excel Version 5 for Windows, enable you to summarize, analyze, and manipulate data in lists and tables. Pivot tables offer more flexible and intuitive analysis of data than the Crosstab Wizard feature in Excel 4, which they replace.

For information about new advanced features, see Que's *Using Excel Version 5 for Windows*, Special Edition.

Using This Book

Excel Version 5 for Windows Quick Reference is organized alphabetically by task. When you are working in Excel and get stuck, or simply want some guidance before you get started, look at the heads at the top of each page to locate the appropriate section. Alternatively, you can use the Index at the back of the book to assist you in locating the information you need.

This Quick Reference covers all of the most often performed tasks in Excel Version 5 for Windows in a quick and concise manner. Whenever you feel that you are in need of a more detailed discussion, turn to Que's

Using Excel Version 5 for Windows, Special Edition for the best and most complete coverage of Excel Version 5 for Windows available.

System Requirements

Before you install Excel Version 5 for Windows, make sure that your computer meets the following hardware, storage, and memory requirements:

- A system with 80286, 80386, or 80486 architecture (an 80386 or 80486 is recommended)

- An EGA, VGA, or other graphics display compatible with Microsoft Windows Version 3.1 or later.

- Microsoft Windows Version 3 or higher, running with DOS Version 3.1 or higher

- At least 4Mb of RAM

- 7Mb of available hard disk storage for Excel Version 5 for Windows program only; 15Mb of available hard disk storage to install the Excel Version 5 for Windows program, additional program features, help and sample files.

The following are optional:

- Printer (any printer supported by Windows 3.0 or 3.1)

- A mouse (highly recommended)

Understanding Windows Basics

Microsoft Windows 3.1 is a powerful, easy-to-use extension to the MS-DOS operating system. If you are new to Windows 3.1, the following basic information should help you get started with Windows 3.1.

One feature that makes Windows 3.1 programs easier to use is the nature of the GUI. Instead of typing commands to start and run a Windows 3.1 program, you can select the program's *application icon* (a small picture that represents the program).

To run an application with a mouse, move the mouse pointer to the icon and double-click the left mouse button.

Running an application with the keyboard is slightly more complex. First, make certain that the window containing the icon is the active window—the window whose border is highlighted. If that window is not active, press Ctrl+Tab until the desired window is active (or select the group window name from the **W**indow menu). Then use the direction keys to highlight the desired application icon (when an application icon is selected, its program name is displayed in reverse video). Finally, press Enter to run the program.

When Excel Version 5 for Windows needs more information about a menu command, a *dialog box* appears. To execute the command, you must complete the dialog box and choose OK or press Enter. You also can cancel a command before it executes by choosing Cancel or pressing Esc to close the dialog box.

You can change the size and position of the Excel window or a worksheet window by using the mouse or the keyboard. You can enlarge a window to fill the entire screen, reduce the window to a smaller size, or shrink the window to an icon.

To enlarge or reduce windows

When you *maximize* the Excel window, it fills the screen. When you maximize the worksheet window and other windows within the Excel window, each window fills the work area of the Excel window. You can enlarge or reduce a window by choosing Ma**x**imize or Mi**n**imize from the Windows menu bar button.

The Zoom Control box on the Standard toolbar also enables you to enlarge or reduce Excel windows. To enlarge or reduce the size of a window, type the percentage in the Zoom Control box or click the down arrow on the right side of the box, and then choose a size from the drop-down list box. You also can click the Minimize or Maximize buttons in the upper right corner of the window.

To move windows

You can move a window or its icon. With the keyboard, choose the **M**ove command from the appropriate Control menu, use the direction keys to relocate the window, and press Enter. Moving a window is easier with the mouse: click the title bar and drag the window to its new location. If the window is minimized, you can click the window's icon and drag it to a new position.

To close windows

Each window has a **C**lose command that enables you to close the worksheet window. To close the window with the mouse, double-click the Control menu box in the upper left corner of the window.

> **Shortcut**
>
> To quickly close the Excel window (or any Windows 3.1 application window), press Alt+F4. To close a worksheet window (or any Windows 3.1 document window), press Ctrl+F4.

If you have made any changes to a window and haven't saved them before you select the **C**lose command, a dialog box prompts you to save any files before closing the window.

To cascade windows

To arrange open windows so that they appear on top of one another, with only the sheet tabs showing, choose **W**indow **A**rrange to display the Arrange Windows dialog box, click the **C**ascade option button, and choose OK. The active window always appears on top. To move between cascaded windows, press Ctrl+Tab or click the appropriate sheet tab at the bottom of the window or the title bar at the top of the window.

To tile windows

To size and arrange all open windows side by side, like floor tiles, choose **W**indow **A**rrange to display the Arrange Windows dialog box, click the **T**iled option button, and then choose OK. The inactive window has a dimmed background. To move between tiled windows, press Ctrl+Tab. You also can click anywhere within the desired window.

To arrange windows horizontally or vertically

To arrange windows horizontally or vertically, choose **W**indow Arrange, click the **H**orizontal or **V**ertical option buttons, and then choose OK. The inactive window is dimmed. To move between windows, press Ctrl+Tab or click the appropriate sheet tab at the bottom of each window.

To choose a window display mode

In addition to the cascade, tile, horizontal, and vertical display-mode options described in the preceding sections, Excel for Windows offers other choices for displaying worksheet windows. You can, for example, split a worksheet window into two panes either verti-cally or horizontally, and maximize a worksheet window to fill the entire work area. With all these choices, you may find it difficult to choose the best display mode for your needs. The following guidelines may help you select the best display mode for your worksheets:

- Maximizing the window provides the largest visible work area.

- Tiling the windows enables you to view portions of several files at the same time.

- Cascading the windows provides a large visible work area for the current window (although not as large as a maximized window) and makes switching between files easy.

- A worksheet can be displayed in only one window at a time. To display two or four views of the same worksheet, choose **W**indow **S**plit.

To switch windows

Excel Version 5 for Windows offers a new way to switch among windows. At the bottom of each worksheet are sheet tabs that you can click to switch to a particular worksheet, chart, or workbook.

To switch among applications

To switch between Windows applications, press Alt+Esc. You also can press Ctrl+Esc to use Windows' Task List dialog box. For more information about the Task List, refer to your Windows documentation.

Shortcut

Press Alt+Tab to switch from application to application in Windows. If the application you switch to is reduced to an icon, the icon restores to a window when you release the Alt key.

The Excel Screen

The Excel Version 5 for Windows screen contains many elements. New to Excel 5 are *sheet tabs*, which enable you to switch among worksheets and charts just by clicking the appropriate sheet tab.

By default, Excel displays two toolbars. The Standard toolbar includes buttons for basic Excel features and the Formatting toolbar includes buttons for formatting changes. The following figure shows an example of the Excel screen.

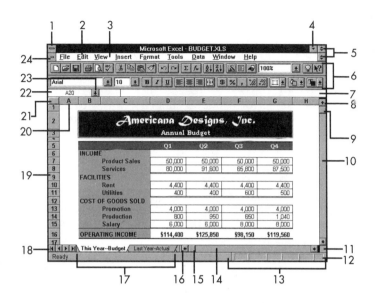

1 Control menu box

2 Title bar

3 Menu bar

4 Minimize button

5 Maximize/Restore buttons

6 Toolbars

7 Formula bar

8 Horizontal split box

9 Vertical scroll box

10 Vertical scroll bar

11 Vertical split box

12 Status bar

13 Status indicators

14 Horizontal scroll bar

15 Horizontal scroll box

16 Tab split box

17 Sheet tabs

18 Tab scrolling buttons

19 Row numbers

20 Column letters

21 Select All button

22 Name box

23 Drop-down name list

24 Workbook Control menu box

Conventions Used in This Book

To make the information as clear to you as possible, this book follows certain conventions. For example, when a keyboard key has a special name, such as F1 or Del, the name appears exactly that way in the text.

When two keys appear together with a plus sign, such as Shift+Ins, press and hold the first key as you press the second key. When two keys appear together without a plus sign, such as End Home, press and release the first key before you press the second key.

Special typefaces in *Excel Version 5 for Windows Quick Reference* include the following:

Type	Meaning
Italics	New terms or phrases when initially defined; function and macro-command syntax.
Boldface	Information you are asked to type.
`Special type`	Direct quotations of words that appear on-screen or in a figure, such as command prompts.

When you must select a series of menu options to initiate a command, they are listed in the order that you select them. For example, **F**ile **S**ave means that you first choose **F**ile and then choose **S**ave.

For easy reference, this book contains special text boxes for shortcut methods to perform the operations discussed in a section. When appropriate, a corresponding toolbar button also appears in the box. The following is an example of a text box which appears in the *Files and File Management* section.

Shortcut

Press Ctrl+S or click the Save button on the Standard toolbar.

Task Reference

Alignment

Alignment options enable you to change the way text appears inside a cell. Text can appear flush with the left, right, top or bottom of a cell. Normally, numbers appear "flush right" while text appears "flush left." You can change the data alignment using the various procedures in this section. An aspect of data alignment includes the data view orientation, which refers to the direction in which the text reads in the cell. Text can read from bottom to top, left to right, top to bottom, or stacked. You can align data with any or all four sides of a cell.

To align data between the left and right sides of a cell

1 Highlight the cell or range containing the data you want to align. All data you highlight will be similarly aligned.

2 Click the Align Left button on the Formatting toolbar to align the data with the left edge of the cell. Click the Align Right button on the Formatting toolbar to align the data with the right edge of the cell. Click the Center button to center the data inside the cell.

See also *Centering*.

To move numbers away from the right edge of a cell

1 Highlight the cell or range containing the data you want to align.

2 Choose Format Cells. The Format Cells dialog box appears.

┌─ **Shortcut** ─────────────────────────────────────┐

You also can press Ctrl+1.

└──┘
---

3 Click the Number tab at the top of the Format Cells dialog box to view the number formats. (This option already may be selected.)

4 Edit the information in the Code text box by adding the characters _M (underscore and M) to the end of each code segment shown in the box. Code segments are separated by semicolons. For example, the code might read #,##0_);(#,##0). Change this to **#,##0_)_M;(#,##0)_M**. If the code reads General, change it to **General_M**.

5 Choose OK.

┌─ **Tip** ──┐

   All number formats that display negative numbers in parentheses also move numbers away from the right edge of the cell. These include the currency and comma formats. Just clicking the Currency button or Comma button (on the Formatting toolbar) to format numeric data might provide the desired space along the right edge.

└──┘

See also *Formatting*.

To align data between the top and bottom of a cell

1 Highlight the cell or range containing the data you want to align.

2 Choose Format Cells or press Ctrl+1. The Format Cells dialog box appears.

3 Click the Alignment tab at the top of the Format Cells dialog box to view the Alignment options.

4 In the Vertical area, choose the Top, Center, or Bottom option button to align the data with the top, center or bottom of the cell. The Justify option works with the Wrap Text check box to make the lines of data fit evenly within the height of the cell.

5 Choose OK.

┌─ **Tip** ─────────────────────────────┐

If needed, you can change the row height of the cells you aligned. This changes the way data fits within the cell. See *Row Heights* for more information.

└──────────────────────────────────────┘

To change the "read" orientation of data

1 Highlight the cell or range containing the data you want to change.

2 Choose Format Cells or press Ctrl+1. The Format Cells dialog box appears.

3 Click the Alignment tab at the top of the Format Cells dialog box to view the Alignment options.

4 In the Orientation area, click the option that shows the orientation you want.

5 Choose OK.

6 If necessary, change the row height or column width of the cells you modified.

To display multiple lines of data within a cell

1 Type into the cell the data you want, and then press Enter. At first, this entry will appear in one long line.

2 Highlight the cell or range containing the data.

3 Choose Format Cells or press Ctrl+1. The Format Cells dialog box appears.

4 Click the Alignment tab at the top of the Format Cells dialog box to view the Alignment options.

5 Check the **Wrap** Text check box.

6 Choose OK. The following figure shows an example of wrapped text.

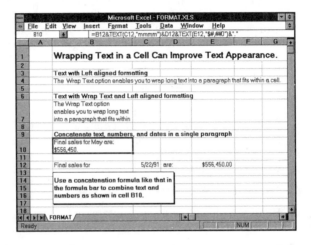

Note

When you change the width of a cell containing wrapped text, the data will adjust to fill the new width of the cell. As a result, the data might not fit from top-to-bottom within the cell and you might have too much or too little space at the bottom. Simply adjust the row height to fix this. See *Row Heights*.

Tip

You might find it easier to format your worksheet text by placing it in a text box rather than trying to format the data within a cell. See *Text Boxes* for more information.

Auditing Worksheets

Excel's audit features are useful tools to help you detect problems in your worksheet formulas. Excel provides an Auditing toolbar that helps you find errors on your worksheets, attach notes to cells, and track problems in your worksheet formulas. Display the toolbar by choosing **View Toolbars** to display the Toolbars dialog box. Check the check box next to Auditing in the **T**oolbars list box, and then choose OK. Following is a description of each button's purpose.

Button	Purpose
Trace Precedents	Draws arrows from all cells that supply values directly to the formula in the active cell (*precedents*).
Remove Precedent Arrows	Deletes a level of precedent tracer arrows from the active worksheet.
Trace Dependents	Draws arrows from the active cell to cells with formulas that use the values in the active cell (*dependents*).
Remove Dependent Arrows	Deletes a level of dependent tracer arrows from the active worksheet.
Remove All Arrows	Deletes all tracer arrows from the active worksheet.
Trace Error	Draws an arrow to an error value in the active cell from cells that might have caused the error.

continues

Button		Purpose
🔳	Attach Note	Displays the Cell Note dialog box so that you can attach text or audio comments to a cell.
ℹ	Show Info Window	Displays the Info window.

Using Tracers to Audit a Worksheet

Tracers enable you to find *precedents*, *dependents*, and errors in any cell in a worksheet. Precedents are cells that are referred to by a formula. Dependents are cells that contain formulas that refer to other cells.

Note

Before using tracers, be sure the Hide All option button is not selected. Choose **T**ools **O**ptions and click the View tab. In the Objects area, the Hide All option button should be white (not selected). Change if necessary and then choose OK.

To trace the precedents of a cell

1 Highlight a cell containing the formula you want to trace. The cell must contain a formula.

2 🔳 Choose **T**ools **A**uditing **T**race Precedents or click the Trace Precedents button on the Auditing toolbar. Tracer arrows appear.

Blue or solid arrows indicate direct precedents of the selected formula.

Red or dotted arrows indicate formulas that refer to error values.

Dashed arrows with a spreadsheet icon at the end refer to external worksheets.

3 As you work with the tracers, you can click the Remove Precedent Arrows button on the Auditing toolbar to remove one level of precedents at a time. Or click the Remove All Arrows button to remove all the tracers.

Tip

Double-click a tracer arrow to select the cell at the point end of the arrow. Double-click again to select the cell at the opposite end. Double-click an external worksheet arrow (with spreadsheet icon at the end) to display the Go To dialog box; select the precedent from the list box and choose OK to go to that sheet.

To trace the dependents of a cell

1 Highlight the cell you want to trace. The cell should be one referenced in a formula.

2 Choose **T**ools **A**uditing **T**race Dependents or click the Trace Dependents button on the Auditing toolbar. Tracer arrows appear. Blue or solid arrows indicate dependents of the selected formula.

3 As you work with the tracers, you can click the Remove Dependent Arrows button on the Auditing toolbar to remove one level of dependents at a time. Or click the Remove All Arrows button to remove all the tracers.

To trace errors in a cell

1 Highlight a cell containing an error value: #DIV/0!, #N/A, #NAME?, #NULL!, #NUM!, #REF!, #VALUE!.

2   Choose **T**ools **A**uditing Trace **E**rror or click the
Trace Error button on the Auditing toolbar.
Tracer arrows appear, pointing to the cells in ques-
tion:

Red or dotted arrows indicate first precedent formula containing an error.

Blue or solid arrows indicate precedents of the first
formula producing an error.

3   Correct the error. The error tracer arrow changes to
a solid precedent arrow.

4   Click the Remove All Arrows button on the Auditing
toolbar or choose **T**ools Auditing Remove **A**ll Arrows from the menu.

> **Tip**
>
> If you want to display an Info window with
> information about the cell, click the Show
> Info button. You see the formula, any notes,
> and formatting of the active cell.

Bolding

See *Formatting*

Borders

Using the border options, you can apply lines and
borders to the worksheet. Borders can be applied to any
of the four sides of a cell. By combining borders across
many cells, you can outline a range or produce a line
across the page. Quick border settings can be applied
using the Border button on the Formatting toolbar. For
more border control, you can use the Format Cells
command with the Border options.

To apply borders to cells or ranges

1 Highlight the cell or range to which you want to apply borders.

2 Click the down arrow beside to the Border button on the Formatting toolbar to view border options.

3 Click the border option you want. Remember that the border applies to each cell in the selected range; if you apply a bottom border, each cell in the range will receive a border at the bottom. The exceptions to this rule are the last three border options, which apply to ranges. (The last two options outline the selected range, for example.) The following figure shows different types of borders.

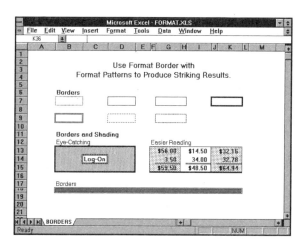

Tip

Once you apply a border by using the Border button, that border selection appears in the face of the Border button. You then can reapply the same border selection by simply clicking the button after highlighting the cell or range you want.

To remove borders from cells or ranges

1 Highlight the cell or range containing the border. If you are in doubt as to which cell the border applies, highlight all possible cells. A border that appears on the left side of one cell might actually be applied to the right side of the cell next to it. When in doubt, highlight both cells.

2 Click the arrow beside the Border button on the Formatting toolbar to reveal the border options.

3 Click the first border option in the list, which contains no border selection.

> ## Tip
>
> You can add to existing border settings by using the border button.

To change the styles and colors of borders

1 Highlight the cells containing borders.

2 Choose Format Cells or press Ctrl+1. The Format Cells dialog box appears.

3 Click the Border tab on the top of the Format Cells dialog box to display the border options.

4 Click the border Style you want. This is the style that will be applied to the selected cells. You can change the existing border style by choosing a different style at this time.

5 Choose a color from the Color drop-down palette.

6 Click the Border options to indicate where you want the colored borders to appear on the selection. If the selection already contains borders, just click the Border options that are already active; this changes the colors of the existing lines. (At this time, you also can change the existing borders by selecting or deselecting the Border options to reflect the desired borders.)

7 Choose OK.

Tip

You can make each border segment (side of cell) a different color. Just choose a Border Style, and then a border **C**olor before clicking the Border option. You can use any combination of styles and colors within a cell.

Caution!

A border attached to the right edge of a cell can look like a border on the left side of the cell beside it. On the worksheet, this makes little difference as long as the border appears where you want it. However, when you highlight a range for printing, only the borders attached to cells in the print area will appear on the printout. If you have a vertical border between columns B and C, for example, the border will appear in the printout of columns A and B only if the border is attached to the right edge of column B.

Buttons

Worksheet buttons are used to run your custom macros. When you click a worksheet button, the macro assigned to that button is invoked and its action applied to the worksheet. Buttons appear in specific locations in a worksheet and are useful for running macros that apply to specific areas of the worksheet. Changing the numbers in a table or the style of a graph are good uses for worksheet buttons. To use a worksheet button completely, you must have a macro recorded you intend to assign to the button. For more information about macros, see *Macros and Custom Controls*.

To draw a button on the worksheet

1 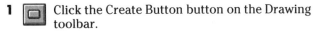 Click the Create Button button on the Drawing toolbar.

2 To create a button of any size, click the worksheet and drag diagonally. This displays the Assign Macro dialog box that enables you to attach a macro to your new button. If you do not have a macro at this time, you either can record one now by clicking the Record button or click the Cancel button to remove this dialog box from the screen. If you remove the dialog box without attaching a macro, you can attach a macro later by following the instructions in *To assign a macro to an existing button*, later in this section.

If the macro you want appears in the Macro Name/ Reference text box, continue with step 3.

3 Click the name of the macro you want, and then choose OK to attach it to the button.

> **Tip**
>
> You can move an existing button by right-clicking it (which produces a shortcut menu). Next, left-click the button's border and drag to move the button. If the button has no macro attached, you can move it simply by dragging with the left mouse button.

To change the name of a button

1 Right-click the button. This displays the button shortcut menu.

2 Left-click the face of the button to remove the shortcut menu.

> **Note**
>
> Right-clicking the button before left-clicking the button tells Excel that you want to edit the button.

3 Click the left mouse button on the button's existing title text, and then drag to highlight the existing title.

4 Type a new title to replace the existing one.

5 Click a cell to deselect the button.

To format the text inside the button

1 Right-click the button to display the shortcut menu.

2 Choose Format Object from the shortcut menu. The Format Object dialog box appears.

3 Click the Font tab to select a font and other type formats for the button's text.

4 Click the Alignment tab to align the text inside the button, including changing the orientation of the button text.

5 Choose OK when finished.

See also *Formatting* and *Alignment*.

┌─ **Note** ─────────────────────────────────

If you choose Format Object from the short-cut menu and only the Font window appears, you probably have the button text highlighted. Click Cancel, click a worksheet cell to deselect the button and text, and then start over by right-clicking the button.

To assign a macro to an existing button

1 Right-click the button to display the shortcut menu.

2 Choose Assign Macro. The Assign Macro dialog box appears.

3 Choose a macro from the **M**acro Name/Reference list box or record a new one with the **R**ecord button.

4 Choose OK to assign the selected macro to the button.

┌─ **Note** ──────────────────────────┐
│ If a macro already is assigned to the button, │
│ these steps will change the macro. │
└─────────────────────────────────────┘

To make a button out of a graphic object

1 Draw or insert a graphic into the worksheet as described in *Pictures*, later in this book.

2 Right-click the graphic object to display the object shortcut menu.

3 Choose Assign Macro from the shortcut menu. The Assign Macro dialog box appears.

4 Choose a macro from the **M**acro Name/Reference box, or record a new one with the **R**ecord button.

5 Choose OK to assign the highlighted macro to the graphic object.

┌─ **Note** ──────────────────────────┐
│ Once a macro is attached to an object, you │
│ must right-click the button to move it or │
│ change its size and shape. First, right-click │
│ the button to select it (this also displays the │
│ shortcut menu). Next, left-click and drag the │
│ button to move it. │
└─────────────────────────────────────┘

See also *Drawing*.

To print buttons with your reports

1 Right-click the button to display the shortcut menu.

2 Choose Format Object. The Format Object dialog box appears.

3 Click the Properties tab.

4 Click the **P**rint Object check box.

5 Choose OK.

6 Choose **F**ile **P**rint to print the button with your report. See also *Printing*.

To delete a button from the worksheet

1 Right-click the button you want to delete. The short-cut menu appears.

2 Choose Clear. The button is deleted.

Calculating Worksheets

Excel normally calculates your worksheets (that is, recalculates the results of your formulas and functions) every time those formulas are affected by changes to information in the worksheet. Some functions, however, require manual recalculation, such as certain time and date functions. If your worksheet is rather large, you may find the automatic recalculation annoying; you can turn off this feature while you work.

To turn off automatic calculation

1 Choose Tools Options. The Options dialog box appears.

2 Click the Calculation tab.

3 In the Calculation area, click the Manual option button.

4 Choose OK.

To calculate the worksheet

1 Choose Tools Options. The Options dialog box appears.

2 Click the Calculation tab.

3 Click the Calc Now (F9) button.

Shortcut

You also can calculate the worksheet at any time by pressing F9. You do not need to be in the dialog box.

To calculate the sum of several columns at once

1   Highlight the blank row of cells directly under the columns; that is, highlight the last cell in each column (forming a row of blank cells below the columns).

2   ⬚Σ⬚   Click the AutoSum button on the Standard toolbar.

Cell Addresses and References

Cell addresses (or *references*) are used to identify specific cells on the worksheet. They identify cells by their row and column headings. References are used in formulas and functions when you calculate the values in cells within the worksheet. Most cell reference topics are covered in *Formulas* later in this book. By default, Excel uses rows and numbers for columns. Instead, you can display row and column numbers, called R1C1 style.

To display R1C1-style references

1   Choose Tools Options. The Options dialog box appears.

2   Click the General tab.

3   In the Reference Style area, click the R1C1 option button to display the R1C1-style references.

4   Choose OK.

Centering

Centering is an important part of worksheet setup. The following procedures show you how to center data within a cell, a heading over columns, and a printed report within the margins of a page.

To center a heading over multiple columns

1 Type a heading at the top of the leftmost column and format the heading the way you want it.

2 Position the cell pointer on the heading cell. Highlight that cell and all the cells above the columns.

3 [icon] Click the Center Across Columns button on the Formatting toolbar.

┌─ **Tip** ──────────────────────────────┐

You can center several headings at once—not just one heading. Suppose that your worksheet displays monthly financial data. Each month requires three columns of data, giving you 36 columns for the year. To center each month heading over its three columns, simply type the month names at the top of the leftmost column of each section. Then highlight the entire row containing the headings and click the Center Across Columns button. All the headings will be centered at once.

└───┘

To center data within a cell

1 Highlight the cell or range containing the data you want to center.

2 [icon] Click the Center button on the Formatting toolbar. The data is centered within the cell.

To print a report in the center of the page

1 Choose **File** Page Set**up**. The Page Setup dialog box appears.

2 Click the Margins tab.

3 In the Center on Page area, click the Horizontally and/or Vertically check boxes. Watch the preview page in the Page Setup dialog box to see how your selections will affect the printout. Notice that the print block is centered within the page margins you establish.

4 When the options are the way you want, click the
Print button to display the Print dialog box.

5 Change printing options as desired, and then choose
OK to print the report.

See also *Alignment* and *Headers and Footers*.

Charts

Charts enable you to visually represent your data.
Relationship to other data points and trends are easier
to see when represented in a chart. Excel provides many
features for creating and formatting a chart. The
ChartWizard leads you step-by-step through the process. Excel enables you to change the default choices
and customize each element of the chart, such as the
font, legend, titles, color, and so on.

Creating Charts

You can use one of two methods to create a chart. You
can use the ChartWizard to create a chart, or you can
create a chart with the Insert Chart command. You can
choose to embed the chart on the worksheet (so that it
appears on the same sheet), or you can place the chart
on a chart sheet in the workbook.

To use the ChartWizard to create a chart

1 Highlight the range you want to chart.

Note

Because you do not want to chart the totals,
do not select the totals in the data range.

> **Tip**
>
> You can select noncontiguous sections to chart, but they must be rectangular in shape. To highlight a noncontiguous range to chart, highlight the first selection with the mouse. Then hold down the Ctrl key and click any additional selections.
>
> If you want to chart only certain data, hide the rows or columns you don't want to chart. You also can outline the data and then collapse it to show only the information you want to chart. See *Outlines*.

2 Click the ChartWizard button on the Standard toolbar.

3 Drag across a blank area of the worksheet to indicate where you want to place the embedded chart. The ChartWizard - Step 1 of 5 dialog box appears.

4 To confirm the selected range, choose Next. Or select a different **R**ange and then choose Next.

> **Tip**
>
> If you change your mind, click the **B**ack button to go backwards through the ChartWizard steps and make changes.

5 In the ChartWizard - Step 2 of 5 dialog box, choose a chart type and then choose Next. The default chart type is column.

6 In the ChartWizard - Step 3 of 5 dialog box, choose a chart format and then choose Next.

7 In the ChartWizard - Step 4 of 5 dialog box, change any of the following and then choose Next:

- Choose the way in which the data series are charted: in **R**ows or in **C**olumns.

- Choose which rows/columns to use as the x-axis text.

- Choose which rows/columns to use for the legend text.

> ## Note
>
> Depending on how you selected to chart the series (in rows or columns), the choices for the x-axis label and legend may be row or column.

8 In the ChartWizard - Step 5 of 5 dialog box, make any of the following changes:

- Choose whether you want to include a legend by clicking the **Y**es or **N**o option button.

- Type the title in the **C**hart Title text box.

- Type axis titles in the Category(**X**) and Value(**Y**) text boxes.

9 Choose **F**inish. The chart appears on-screen.

To create a chart with the Insert Chart command

1 Highlight the range you want to chart.

2 Choose Insert Chart.

3 From the Chart shortcut menu, choose **O**n This Sheet or **A**s New Sheet.

4 If you chose to insert the chart on the current worksheet, drag across a blank area of the worksheet to indicate where you want to place the chart. If you chose to place the chart on a separate sheet, skip this step.

5 To confirm the selected range, choose Next. Or select a different **R**ange and then choose Next.

Tip

If you change your mind, click the **B**ack option button to go backwards through the ChartWizard steps and make changes.

---

6 In the ChartWizard - Step 2 of 5 dialog box, choose a chart type and then choose Next. The default chart type is column.

7 In the ChartWizard - Step 3 of 5 dialog box, choose a chart format and then choose Next.

8 In the ChartWizard - Step 4 of 5 dialog box, change any of the following and then choose Next:

- Choose the way in which the data series are charted: in **R**ows or in **C**olumns.

- Choose which rows/columns to use as the x-axis text.

- Choose which rows/columns to use for the legend text.

Note

Depending on how you selected to chart the series (in rows or columns), the choices for the x-axis label and legend may be row or column.

---

9 In the ChartWizard - Step 5 of 5 dialog box, make any of the following changes:

- Choose whether you want to include a legend by clicking the **Y**es or **N**o option button.

- Type the title in the **C**hart Title text box.

- Type axis titles in the Category(**X**) and Value(**Y**) text boxes.

10 Choose **F**inish. The chart appears on-screen.

To move a chart

1 Click the chart you want to move. Black selection handles appear around the border of the chart, indicating that it is selected.

2 With the mouse pointer inside the chart, drag the chart to a new location and then release the mouse button.

To delete a chart

1 Click the chart you want to delete.

2 Press Delete. The chart is deleted.

Editing Chart Data

As you edit a worksheet, you may need to make changes to your chart—add data, remove data, change data, and so on. Excel also enables you to change the charted range.

To add data to a chart

1 In the worksheet, highlight the data you want to add.

2 If the worksheet and chart are on the same sheet, drag (with mouse pointer touching the side of the data box) the data onto the chart. If the Paste Special dialog box appears, instruct Excel to paste the data as a new series or new points. Also, specify whether the Y values are in rows or columns. Choose any other options that apply. Choose OK.

If the worksheet and chart sheet are separate, choose **E**dit **C**opy or press Ctrl+C, switch to the chart sheet, click the chart, and choose **E**dit **P**aste or press Ctrl+V.

Shortcut ───────────────────

  You also can use the Copy and Paste buttons on the Standard toolbar.

To remove data from a chart

1 Double-click the chart.

2 Double-click the data series you want to delete.

3 Press Delete. The series is removed from the chart, but the chart data still remains in the worksheet. To delete individual data points from a series, delete the data from the worksheet, or highlight a different range to chart.

To change underlying chart data

1 Double-click the chart.

2 Click the data point you want to change. When a single data point is selected, black selection handles appear along the borders of the area.

3 Drag the data point up or down. The resulting worksheet data is updated to reflect the change.

Note

If the Goal Seek dialog box is displayed, the value of the marker you are changing is a formula. The Set cell text box shows the cell references containing the formula for the data point. The To value text box shows the value to which you dragged the data point. Change the value, if you want. Click the By changing cell text box. Type the cell reference or click the cell whose value should change to enable the data point to reach the specified value. This cell must be a cell on which the formula depends, directly or indirectly. Choose OK to display the Goal Seel Status dialog box. Choose OK to make the change in the chart and worksheet.

Editing Chart Elements

If you don't like the appearance of the chart, you can change the placement of the elements. You can arrange the data points so that they are overlapped. You also can change the frame used and add drawings.

To select chart elements

See *Selecting*

To move elements within the chart window

1 Double-click the chart.

2 Select the chart element you want to move.

3 Drag the element to a new location.

To draw inside a chart window

1 Click the Drawing button on the Standard toolbar to display the Drawing toolbar.

2 Click the drawing button you want to use.

3 Click and drag to create the object on the chart.

┌─ **Note** ──────────────────────────────
│ For more information, see *Drawing*.
└───

To format the chart frame

1 Click the chart to select the frame.

2 Choose Format Object or press Ctrl+1. The Format Object dialog box appears.

3 Click the Patterns tab at the top of the Format Object dialog box.

4 To change the border, choose the Custom option button. Then choose the Style, Color, and Weight by clicking the drop-down arrow and then clicking the option you want.

5 To create a Shadow or use Round corners, click these check boxes.

6 To change the pattern, click the **P**attern drop-down list box and then click the pattern you want.

7 Choose OK.

Customizing the Chart Type

As you work with the chart and data, you might decide that a different chart type is better. Excel offers several chart types and formats to choose from. You can select the chart type as you create the chart. Or if you already created the chart, you easily can change the chart type.

To change the chart type with the Chart Type button

1 Click the chart to select it.

2 [icon] Click the drop-down arrow next to the Chart Type button on the Chart toolbar.

3 Click the new chart type you want.

To change the chart type with the Format command

1 Double-click the chart.

2 Choose Format Chart Type. The Chart Type dialog box appears.

3 Choose the 2-D or 3-D option button.

4 Choose the chart type you want.

5 If you want to see additional chart subtypes, click the **O**ptions button and then choose the chart you want from the **S**ubtype area.

> **Tip**
>
> To create a stacked or 100% chart, follow step 5 and choose the chart from the **S**ubtype area.

6 Choose OK.

To change the order of the data series

1 Double-click the chart.

2 Choose Format 1 *Column* Group. The Format Group dialog box appears.

> ┌─ **Note** ──────────────────────────
> The word in italic will vary depending on the type of chart with which you are working. If you are working with a pie chart, for example, the menu will display *Pie Group*.

3 Click the Series Order tab.

4 Click the series you want to move, and then click the Move Up or Move Down buttons.

5 Choose OK.

To overlap and change the space between the data series

1 Double-click the chart.

2 Choose Format 1 *Column* Group to display the Format Group dialog box.

3 Click the Options tab.

4 To overlap the series, enter a value in the Overlap spin box, or click the up or down arrows to choose a value. (You can only overlap 2-D charts.)

5 To change the width between the data series, click in the Gap Width spin box and type a value, or click the up or down arrows to choose a value.

6 Choose OK.

To make each plot point a different series color

1 Double-click the chart.

2 Choose Format 1 *Column* Group to display the Format Group dialog box.

3 Click the Options tab.

4 Check the Vary Colors by Point check box.

5 Choose OK.

To create a combination chart

1 Double-click the chart.

2 Click the series you want to chart differently.

3 Choose Format Chart Type to display the Chart Type dialog box.

4 Click the chart type you want to use for this series.

> **Tip**
>
> If you want to customize this series, click the Options button. Click the sheet tab you want, make the changes, and then choose OK.

5 Choose OK.

To assign data series to different Y-Axes

1 Double-click the chart.

2 Choose Format 1 *Column* Group. The Format Group dialog box appears.

3 Click the Axis tab.

4 Choose whether to plot a Primary axis or Secondary axis by clicking the appropriate option button.

5 Choose OK.

To create depth on 3-D charts

1 Double-click a 3-D chart.

2 Choose Format 1 3-D *Column* Group. The Format Group dialog box appears.

3 Click the Options tab.

4 Enter a new value for the **G**ap Depth, **C**hart Depth, or Gap **W**idth. You can type the value in the spin box or use the up or down arrows to select a value.

5 Choose OK.

To change the 3-D chart view

1 Double-click a 3-D chart.

2 Click the plot area.

3 Position the mouse pointer on a corner handle of the 3-D plot area.

4 Drag the mouse to change the perspective.

To explode a pie wedge

1 Double-click the chart.

2 Click the plot area.

3 Click the pie wedge you want to explode.

4 Drag the pie wedge away from the pie.

Customizing Chart Series

A chart series is a set of data points and each series appears in a different color or pattern. Excel 5 enables you to change the patterns used to represent each series, as well as the legend and the series name. You also can add series data labels.

To change series patterns

1 Double-click the chart.

2 Click the data series you want to change.

3 Choose Format Selected Data Series or press Ctrl+1. The Format Data Series dialog box appears.

> **Tip**
>
> You also can double-click the series you want to change to display the Format Data Series dialog box.

4 Click the Patterns tab at the top of the Format Data Series dialog box.

5 Choose the border and pattern (or line and marker) you want to use for this series.

6 To invert negative values, click the Invert if Negative check box.

7 Choose OK.

To change the X values

1 Double-click the chart.

2 Click the data series you want to change.

3 Choose Format Selected Data Series or press Ctrl+1. The Format Data Series dialog box appears.

4 Click the X Values tab at the top of the Format Data Series dialog box.

5 Click the **X** values text box, and then highlight the cells in the worksheet that contain the values you want to use.

6 Choose OK.

To change the series name and data range

1 Double-click the chart.

2 Click the data series you want to change.

3 Choose Format Selected Data Series or press Ctrl+1. The Format Data Series dialog box appears.

4 Click the Names and Values tab at the top of the Format Data Series dialog box.

5 Click the **N**ame text box and click the cell in the worksheet that contains the name you want to use, or enter a name.

6 Click the **Y** Values text box, and then click the cell in the worksheet that contains the name you want to use. You also can enter a name.

7 Choose OK.

To add series data labels

1 Double-click the chart.

2 Click the data series you want to change.

3 Choose Format Selected Data Series or press Ctrl+1. The Format Data Series dialog box appears.

4 Click the Data Labels tab at the top of the Format Data Series dialog box.

5 Choose what you want to show, such as the value, percent, label, label and percent. (Depending on the chart type, some of the options may not be available.)

> ## Tip
> To show just one value, such as the key value, apply the labels to the series, click each of the values you want to delete, and then press Delete.

6 To show a small legend key next to the values, check the Show Legend Key Next to Label check box.

7 Choose OK.

Customizing the Plot Area, Walls, and Chart Area

The plot area in a 2-D chart is the area bounded by the axes (basically, the background grid). The plot area for a 3-D chart includes the category names, tick-mark labels, and axis titles. 3-D charts also contain walls and a floor. The chart area is the entire chart, including legends.

To change the colors and patterns of the plot area

1 Double-click the chart.

2 Click the plot area to select it.

3 Choose Format Selected Plot Area or press Ctrl+1. The Format Plot Area dialog box appears.

> **Tip**
>
> You also can double-click the plot area to display the Format Plot area dialog box.

4 Choose the border and pattern options you want.

5 Choose OK.

To change the colors and patterns of the 3-D chart walls

1 Double-click the 3-D chart.

2 Click the chart walls to select them.

3 Choose Format Selected Walls or press Ctrl+1. The Format Walls dialog box appears.

> **Tip**
>
> Double-click the chart wall to display the Format Walls dialog box.

4 Choose the border and pattern options you want.

5 Choose OK.

To change the colors and patterns of the chart area

1 Double-click the chart.

2 Click the chart area to select it.

3 Choose Format Selected Chart Area or press Ctrl+1. The Format Chart Area dialog box appears.

> **Tip**
>
> Double-click the chart area to display the Format Chart Area dialog box.

4 Click the Patterns tab.

5 Choose the border and pattern options you want.

6 Choose OK.

To change the chart's default font

1 Double-click the chart.

2 Click the chart area to select it.

3 Choose Format Selected Chart Area or press Ctrl+1. The Format Chart Area dialog box appears.

4 Click the Font tab.

5 Choose the font, style, size, color, and effects you want.

6 Choose OK.

Customizing Chart Axes

The y axis is the vertical axis on a chart. The x axis is the horizontal axis. You can customize these axes so that the tick marks and values appear as you want.

To change the axis line and tick marks

1 Double-click the chart.

2 Click the axis you want to change.

3 Choose Format Selected Axis or press Ctrl+1. The Format Axis dialog box appears.

> **Tip**
>
> Double-click the axis to display the Format Axis dialog box.

4 Click the Patterns tab.

5 To change the line style, click Custom in the Axis box, choose the **S**tyle, **C**olor, and **W**eight by clicking each drop-down arrow, and then clicking the option you want.

6 Choose the placement of the major and minor tick marks (None, Inside, Outside, or Cross) by clicking the appropriate option buttons.

7 Choose OK.

To change the position of the axis labels

1 Double-click the chart.

2 Click the axis you want to change.

3 Choose Format Selected Axis or press Ctrl+1.
The Format Axis dialog box appears.

4 Click the Patterns tab.

5 Choose where to place the tick-mark labels by clicking the None, High, Low, or Next to Axis option buttons in the Tick-Mark Labels area.

6 Choose OK.

To change the axis label font

1 Double-click the chart.

2 Click the axis you want to change.

3 Choose Format Selected Axis or press Ctrl+1.
The Format Axis dialog box appears.

4 Click the Font tab.

5 Choose the font, style, size, color, and effects you
want.

6 Choose OK.

To change the numeric format of axis values

1 Double-click the chart.

2 Click the axis you want to change.

3 Choose Format Selected Axis or press Ctrl+1.
The Format Axis dialog box appears.

4 Click the Number tab.

5 Choose the numeric format you want to use.

6 Choose OK.

To change the alignment of axis label text

1 Double-click the chart.

2 Click the axis you want to change.

3 Choose Format Selected Axis or press Ctrl+1.
The Format Axis dialog box appears.

4 Click the Alignment tab.

5 Choose the Orientation you want for the label text.

6 Choose OK.

To change X-Axis scale

1 Double-click the chart.

2 Click the x-axis.

3 Choose Format Selected Axis or press Ctrl+1.
The Format Axis dialog box appears.

4 Click the Scale tab.

5 Enter a number (default is 1) in the following three
text boxes:

Value (Y) Axis Crosses at Category Number

Number of Categories between Tick-Mark Labels

Number of Categories between Tick Marks

6 Choose any of the following check boxes:

Value (Y) Axis Crosses between Categories

Categories in Reverse Order

Value (Y) Axis Crosses at Maximum Category

Note

Depending on the chart type, these options
will vary.

7 Choose OK.

To change Y-Axis scale

1 Double-click the chart.

2 Click the y-axis.

3 Choose Format Selected Axis or press Ctrl+1.
The Format Axis dialog box appears.

4 Click the Scale tab.

5 Edit any of the following options by clicking the
appropriate text box:

Enter the Minimum value you want for the scale.

Enter the Maximum value you want for the scale.

Enter the Major Unit you want to use.

Enter the Minor Unit you want to use.

Enter the value at which you want the Category (X)
Axis to Cross this axis. Choose the auto check boxes
for any of the preceding options to enable Excel to
select the values.

> ┌ **Note** ─────────────────────────
> Depending on the chart type, these options
> will vary.

6 Click in any of the following check boxes if you want
to activate the option:

Logarithmic Scale

Values in Reverse Order

Category (X) Axis Crosses at Maximum Value

7 Choose OK.

Customizing Chart Titles

You can add a title that explains the purpose of your
chart. You also can add text along the x and y axes. You
can format these titles any way you choose.

To insert chart titles

1 Double-click the chart.

2 Choose Insert Titles. The Titles dialog box appears.

3 Choose the check boxes for each type of title you want displayed.

4 Choose OK. Excel places a box on the chart for each title selected.

5 Type the text and press Enter. If you chose more than one check box, click each title and enter text for each one.

To change the font of chart titles

1 Double-click the chart.

2 Click the title you want to change so that it is selected.

3 Choose Format Selected Chart Title or press Ctrl+l. The Format Title dialog box appears.

Tip

Double-click the chart title to display the Format Title dialog box.

---

4 Click the Font tab.

5 Choose the font you want from the Font list box. Choose the style from the Font Style list box. To change the size, click the size you want in the Size list box. (See also *Fonts*.)

6 Choose OK.

To change the chart title alignment

1 Double-click the chart.

2 Click the title you want to change so that it is selected.

3 Choose Format Selected Chart Title or press Ctrl+l. The Format Title dialog box appears.

4 Click the Alignment tab.

5 Choose the horizontal alignment (**L**eft, **C**enter, **R**ight, or **J**ustify), vertical alignment (**T**op, **C**enter, **B**ottom, or **J**ustify), and the orientation you want.

6 Choose OK.

To change the chart title patterns and colors

1 Double-click the chart.

2 Click the title you want to change.

3 Choose Format Selected Chart Title or press Ctrl+l. The Format Title dialog box appears.

4 Click the Pattern tab.

5 Choose the border and area options you want.

6 Choose OK.

Customizing the Chart Legend

When you create a chart, a legend is added by default. If you don't like the default colors, placement, font, and border, you can change them.

To change legend fonts

1 Double-click the chart.

2 Click the legend to select it.

3 Choose Format Selected Legend or press Ctrl+l. The Format Legend dialog box appears.

> **Tip**
> Double-click the legend to display the Format Legend dialog box.

4 Click the Font tab.

5 Choose the font you want from the **Font** list box. Choose the style from the **Font** Style list box. To change the size, click the size you want in the **Size** list box. (See also *Fonts.*)

6 Choose OK.

To change legend position

1 Double-click the chart.

2 Click the legend to select it.

3 Choose **Format Selected Legend** or press Ctrl+l. The Format Legend dialog box appears.

4 Click the Placement tab.

5 Choose the placement you want by clicking an op- tion button in the Type area.

> ## Tip
> You also can drag the legend to the place you want it.

6 Choose OK.

To change legend colors and patterns

1 Double-click the chart.

2 Click the legend to select it.

3 Choose **Format Selected Legend** or press Ctrl+l. The Format Legend dialog box appears.

4 Click the Patterns tab.

5 Choose the pattern you want from the **Pattern** drop- down list box.

6 Choose OK.

To change the legend box properties

1 Double-click the chart.

2 Click the legend to select it.

3 Choose Format Selected Legend or press Ctrl+l. The Format Legend dialog box appears.

4 Click the Patterns tab.

5 Choose the Custom option button in the Border area.

6 Choose the Style, Color, and Weight you want to use for the legend box by clicking each down arrow and then clicking option you want.

7 If you want a drop shadow for the box, choose the Shadow check box.

8 Choose OK.

Closing Files

See *Files and File Management*

Color

Excel uses color in many ways. You can use different colors for different types of data on the page, you can use color as a background for your data and you can use color in your charts and graphs. Excel 5's new color selection buttons make choosing colors easy. You also can change the various colors offered in Excel and design palettes of your own for special applications.

Text Color

Excel enables you to change the color of text and values inside cells. You have 56 basic colors from which to choose and you can apply colors to individual cells or ranges. Besides displaying colors on-screen, you can print your worksheets in color if you have a color printer—or use the colors to produce gray shades on black and white printers.

To change the color of text

1 Highlight the cells that contain the data you want to color.

2 Click down arrow next to the Font Color button on the Formatting toolbar.

3 Choose a color from the Font Color palette.

Tip

When you choose a color from the Font Color palette, the selected color appears as the new button face. If you simply click the face of the button, you will apply the color again (the color on the face). This feature enables you to reapply colors without selecting them from the palette repeatedly.

To print text in color

1 Choose File Page Setup. The Page Setup dialog box.

2 Click the Sheet tab.

3 Click to remove the X from the Black and White check box in the Print area.

4 Choose OK or choose Print to print the report.

Note

To print in color, you must have a color printer on-line and selected in the current printer list. To add a new printer to the Windows printer list, use the Printer settings in the Windows Control Panel. Choose this printer before attempting these steps. If you print in color to a black and white printer, colors will appear as gray shades. If you print in color to a black and white PCL printer, all colors will print as black.

Cell Color

You can change the background color within cells or ranges to get various effects on the worksheet. By combining the cell color with text color, you can get some attractive color presentations. You might want to use cell color to highlight areas of your worksheet or to call attention to certain information.

To apply colors to cells

1 Highlight the range you want to color. This can be a single cell or the entire worksheet.

2 Click the down arrow next to the Color button on the Formatting toolbar.

3 Choose a color from the palette.

> **Note**
>
> White and None are not the same. If you want to remove color from the worksheet, choose the None option at the top of the color list.

> **Tip**
>
> When you choose a color from the Color palette, the selected color appears as the new button face. If you simply click the face of the button, you will apply the color again (the color on the face). This feature enables you to reapply colors without selecting them from the palette repeatedly.

To apply patterns to cells

1 Highlight the cells you want to change.

2 Choose Format Cells or press Ctrl+1. The Format Cells dialog box appears.

3 Click the Patterns tab.

4 Click the Pattern drop-down list. The list provides 18 different patterns at the top, plus the standard 56 colors at the bottom.

5 Click the patterns to apply this pattern to the selected range.

6 Click the **P**attern drop-down list again and choose a color for the pattern you selected.

7 Choose OK. The following figure illustrates some of the available shades and patterns.

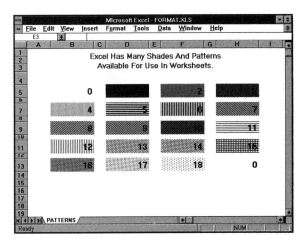

Numeric Values and Color

You can make Excel change the color of the numeric values in your worksheet based on their values. For example, all values under 100 can be displayed in blue, all negative values can be displayed in red, while values 100 and over appear in black. This is useful for your formulas, since you may not know the value produced by the formula ahead of time. With a custom number format, the value produced by the formula will cause the correct color to appear.

To change colors based on the values in cells

1 Highlight the desired cells. These cells should contain numeric values that will change colors based on your conditions.

2 Choose Format Cells or press Ctr+1. The Format Cells dialog box appears.

3 Click the Number tab. The following figure shows the Number tab in the Format Cells dialog box.

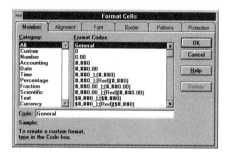

4 In the Category list box, click Custom.

5 Click the Code text box and enter the following format:

[Red] [<0 - (#,##0.00) ; [Blue] [<100]#,##0.00_) ; [Black]#,##0.00_)

Conditions are separated by semicolons, thus, in this example, negative numbers [<0] will appear in Red enclosed in parentheses, numbers under 100 [<100] will appear in Blue, and all other numbers will appear in Black, in the numeric format illustrated. When typing the code, replace the color markers with a color of your choice. (Colors include [Red], [Blue], [Black], [White], [Green], [Magenta], and [Cyan].) Also, replace the conditions to modify the range of numbers to be displayed in a given color. In this example, all the numbers are formatted with two decimal places; you can change the format, or you can use the currency format. The sample example in the currency format would be entered as follows:

[Red] [<0] - ($#,##0.00) ; [Blue] [<100]$#,##0.00_) ; [Black]$#,##0.00-)

6 Choose OK.

┌─ **Tip** ──────────────────────────────┐

The custom number format you created will be added to the Custom and Number (or Currency) categories and appear in the Format Codes list box in the Format Cells dialog box. You can choose this format for any cells in your worksheet.

└───┘

See also *Formatting.*

Palettes

Excel uses a color palette for the various color choices available in your worksheets. The same colors are available throughout Excel, such as in the Color and Text Color buttons on the toolbar. The standard palette uses 56 different colors and you can change the palette at any time. The following procedures show you how to control Excel's color palettes.

To change colors in the color palette

1 Choose **T**ools **O**ptions. The Options dialog box appears.

2 Click the Color tab. Note that different pieces of the palette are automatically used as colors for charts. If you want to change the default chart colors, you can do so by changing the appropriate row of the palette. Similarly, if you change any colors in the Chart Fills row, it will affect your default chart fills. For more information about chart fills and colors, see *Charts* earlier in this book.

3 Double-click the color in the palette you want to change. The Color Picker dialog box appears.

4 Click in the color spectrum box to choose a basic color. You also may click in the Luminance bar to vary the color you have selected. Numeric values fill the entry boxes, identifying the color you have chosen. You may change the numeric values to experiment with the color mix.

5 When you are satisfied with your new color, choose OK, and then choose OK again to return to the worksheet.

To copy custom color palettes between worksheets

1 Open the worksheet that contains the colors you want to copy into the current worksheet. When the worksheet is open, switch back to the first worksheet by using the **W**indow menu or pressing Ctrl+F6.

2 Choose **T**ools **O**ptions. The Options dialog box appears.

3 Click the Color tab.

4 Choose the name of the worksheet you want from the worksheets listed in the **C**opy Colors from drop-down list. Excel copies the colors in the worksheet you choose. Only worksheets that are currently open will appear in this list.

5 Choose OK. The color palette in the current worksheet will change to match the one in the worksheet you specified in step 4.

> ## Note
>
> If you copy new colors into the current worksheet or modify the existing colors, you can return to the default color palette by clicking the **R**eset button in the Color tab of the Options dialog box.

Column Widths

Excel enables you to change the width of any column in the worksheet. When you type data into a cell, you might exceed the existing width and want to expand the column—or you might want to narrow the column to better fit small entries. You can set column widths individually or in groups. You also can fit column widths automatically to the largest entry in the column.

To change the width of a column

1 Locate the right border (or edge) of the column you want to change and follow it to the top of the worksheet into the column heading area. When you move the mouse pointer to that area, the pointer shape changes to a thick crosshair.

2 Click the right column heading border and drag the mouse to the right to expand the column; drag to the left to reduce the column.

Tip

To hide the column, drag past the left column border. See *Hiding Data*.

Note

When you enter text that exceeds the width of a column, Excel spills over the text in the adjacent column (provided that the adjacent cell contains no data). If the adjacent cell contains data, your entry will be truncated at the edge of the cell. The entire entry is still intact, but does not appear. When you enter numbers (or format numbers) that exceed the width of the column, Excel displays ### signs in the cell to indicate that you should expand the width of the column.

To automatically set the width to match the data

1 Locate the right column border in the column heading section of the worksheet, as described in the previous procedure.

2 Double-click the border. The column changes to best fit the data in it. Its width will reflect the largest entry in the column.

> ┌ **Note** ─────────────────────────
>
> After changing a column with the automatic width procedure, if you enter data into the column that exceeds the current width, you will have to readjust the column width.

To change the widths of multiple columns

1 Click the heading (column letter) of the first column in the group, and then drag to highlight other adjacent columns.

> ┌ **Tip** ─────────────────────────
>
> To add nonadjacent columns to the group, press and hold down the Ctrl key and click the other columns you want to add.

2 Double-click the right border of the column heading (column letter) of any of the selected columns. This sets the widths of all columns to match their largest entries. Alternatively, you can adjust the width of any one of the selected columns as described in a previous section *To change the width of a column*. This sets the widths of all selected columns to the same width.

To set a new default column width

1 Choose Format Column Standard Width. The Standard Width dialog box appears.

2 Enter the new width for standard columns. Width is measured in characters, based on the width of a single numeric character in the default font. You can change the default font as described in *Fonts*.

3 Choose OK.

Consolidation

Consolidation enables you to take blocks of data found in several different worksheets (or in different pages of the same workbook) and combine their values into a single, summary range in any workbook. Suppose that you have monthly sales data in your workbook; each of twelve workbook pages displays the sales totals for the month. At the end of the year, you want to consolidate the monthly reports into a summary report that adds the values in all twelve monthly pages. Rather than copying and pasting data from the monthly sheets, or building formulas on the summary sheet that refer to all twelve other sheets, you can use consolidation features to automatically total the data and place the totals in the summary worksheet. The consolidation process is described in the following sections.

> **Note**
>
> The consolidation areas should be of equal size and shape.

To consolidate data across several worksheets or worksheet pages

1 On a blank worksheet page, or in a blank area of the worksheet, highlight a cell. The consolidated report will appear on this page, starting at the highlighted cell.

2 Choose **D**ata Co**n**solidate. The Consolidate dialog box appears.

3 Highlight the first area you want to consolidate. You can click the worksheet and drag to highlight the area, and you can switch worksheets using the sheet tabs. The reference you select appears in the **Refer-ence** text box in the Consolidate dialog box. When highlighting the range, do not include row and col-umn text in the source areas—just numeric data. Also, any formulas included in the source area are used only as values; that is, only the values in the cells will be used in the consolidation.

Tip

You can consolidate from external work-books as well as pages within the same workbook. To access a different workbook, click the **B**rowse button and identify the workbook using the file selection dialog box that appears. When the name of the work-book appears in the dialog box, add a refer-ence to the desired range inside that work-book.

You also can use range names to identify any source area from any page. If the range you want to consolidate is named, just type the range name in place of the range refer-ence in the Reference entry box.

---

4 When the range you want is highlighted, click the **A**dd button. The reference will appear in the bottom portion of the dialog box.

5 Repeat steps 3 and 4 to highlight the next area in the consolidation. Continue until all areas are high-lighted.

6 Choose a function from the **F**unction drop-down list. By default, Excel assumes that you want to SUM the data across the selected range, but you can consoli-date to form averages or other results.

7 Check the Create Links to **S**ource Data check box if you want the summary report to automatically cre-ate linking formulas to the source data. This way, if you change the data inside any of the source ranges, the summary report will change automatically.

The consolidation report, in essence, becomes permanent. Each cell in the summary report will contain a linking formula.

8 Choose OK to complete the consolidation.

To consolidate selected rows and columns from several worksheets or pages

1 On a blank worksheet page, or in a blank area of the worksheet, type the row and column text you want to consolidate from the source ranges. Be sure to type the text exactly as they appear in the source data ranges. If your source ranges contain listings of all products and their sales totals for each month, for example, you might decide to consolidate only certain products from the list.

2 Highlight the row or column labels you entered in step 1 If you entered both row and column labels, highlight a block that includes them all. The consolidated report will appear on this page, starting at the highlighted range.

> ┌─ **Note** ─────────────────────
> All areas should have identical row and column labels.

3 Choose **D**ata Co**n**solidate from the menu to display the Consolidate dialog box.

4 Highlight the first area to be consolidated. You can click the worksheet and drag to highlight the area, and you can switch worksheets clicking the sheet tabs. The reference you select appears in the **R**eference text box in the Consolidate dialog box. When highlighting the range, be sure to include row and column text in the source areas as well as the numeric data. Any formulas included in the source area will be used only as values; that is, only the values in the cells will be used in the consolidation.

5 When the range you want is highlighted, click the **A**dd option button. The reference will appear in the bottom portion of the dialog box.

6 Repeat steps 4 and 5 to highlight the next area in the consolidation. Continue until all areas are high-lighted.

7 Choose a function from the **F**unction drop-down list. By default, Excel assumes that you want to SUM the data across the selected range, but you can consoli-date to form averages or other results.

8 Check the Create Links to **S**ource Data check box if you want the summary report to automatically cre-ate linking formulas to the source data. This way, if you change the data inside any of the source ranges, the summary report will change automatically. The consolidation report, in essence, becomes perma-nent. Each cell in the summary report will contain a linking formula.

9 If you entered row text in step 1, check the **T**op Row check box in the Use Labels In area. If you entered column text in step 1, click the **L**eft Column check box.

10 Choose OK to complete the consolidation.

> ┌─ **Tip** ────────────────────────────
> Excel formats the numbers in the summary report automatically using the number for-mat from the first source data range that appears in the All References list box. If this range uses currency formats, then the sum-mary report will do the same.

Converting

Excel enables you to convert different types of data in your worksheets. You can open worksheet created by other programs and convert them into Excel work-sheets. You can convert formulas into the values they display. And you can convert graphic objects into bitmapped graphics.

To convert formulas into values

1 Highlight the cell or range containing the formulas you want to convert.

2 Choose Edit Copy.

┌─ **Shortcut** ──────────────────────────────┐

  Press Ctrl+C or click the Copy button on the Standard toolbar.

└───┘

3 Highlight the range into which you want the converted values to appear. To replace the original formulas with the values, choose the same cell or range containing the formulas themselves.

4 Choose Edit Paste Special to display the Paste Special dialog box.

5 Click the Values option button.

6 Choose OK.

To convert Lotus 1-2-3 or other worksheets into Excel worksheets

1 Choose File Open. The Open dialog box appears.

┌─ **Shortcut** ──────────────────────────────┐

  Click the Open button on the Standard toolbar.

└───┘

2 In the List Files of Type drop-down list, locate the type of file you want, such as a Lotus 1-2-3 file, text file, or other. Choose the type that matches your source file.

3 Locate the file in the File Name list. You can change directories using the Directories list if desired.

4 Click the file and choose OK, or double-click the file in the File Name list.

5 Excel may simply convert the file to an Excel worksheet, or you may see additional options on-screen. Follow the directions on-screen to complete the process.

> ┌─ **Note** ─────────────────────────
> Excel's conversion filters are selected dur-
> ing the installation process. If you chose
> not to install the filters when you installed
> Excel, you can return to the setup program
> and add them at any time. Use the **A**dd/
> Remove command button in the Microsoft
> Excel 5.0 Setup dialog box to do so.

To change data to graphic objects

1 Highlight the data you want to copy.

2 Press and hold down the Shift key and choose **E**dit **C**opy Picture. The Copy Picture dialog box appears.

3 Choose either the Pic**t**ure or **B**itmap option button in the Format area.

4 Choose OK.

5 Click the mouse where you want to place the object. (This can be a different location on the sheet, a dif-ferent sheet, or a different workbook.)

6 Choose **E**dit Paste **S**pecial. The Paste Special dialog box appears.

7 Choose a format from the **A**s list box, and then choose OK.

> ┌─ **Note** ─────────────────────────
> You can manipulate the object as any other
> graphic object in Excel; however, the object
> contains links to the source area of the
> worksheet.

To change graphic objects to bitmapped graphics

1 Click the object to select it.

2 Press and hold the Shift key down and choose **E**dit **C**opy Picture. The Copy Picture dialog box appears.

3 Choose the **B**itmap option button in the Format area.

4 Choose OK.

5 Open another program or another sheet of the workbook and paste the picture into that document. If
you are pasting back into Excel, choose the **E**dit
Paste **S**pecial command to display the Paste Special
dialog box. Choose a format from the **A**s list box,
and then choose OK.

Copying

In Excel, you can copy data within a worksheet, between
worksheets, between workbooks, or even between Excel
and another program. As you copy different types of
data, notice various options available for your conve-
nience. The following procedures describe how to copy
different types of data in Excel.

To copy data to another location on the same page

1 Highlight the cell or range you want to copy.

2 Press and hold down the Ctrl key, and then click the
mouse pointer on the border edge of the highlighted
range. The pointer should turn into an arrow before
you click.

3 Hold the mouse button down and drag the selection
in the worksheet to the location you want.

4 Release the mouse button.

┌─ **Note** ─────────────────────────────┐
│ If the selection contains formulas, the   │
│ copies of those formulas will adjust relative │
│ to the new location.   │
└────────────────────────────────────┘

**To copy data between worksheets, workbooks, or
programs using the Clipboard**

1 Highlight the cell or range you want to copy.

2 Choose **E**dit **C**opy.

⌐ **Shortcut** ─────────────────

 Press Ctrl+C or click the Copy button on the Standard toolbar.

3 Select the cell marking the upper left corner of the destination range. The data will be copied to this location and fill cells down and to the right as needed. You can highlight a cell on any sheet in any workbook. You also can move to a different program by using the Windows Task Switch dialog box (Ctrl+Esc), and then position the cursor where you want the data to appear.

4 Choose **Edit P**aste.

⌐ **Shortcut** ─────────────────

 Press Ctrl+V or click the Paste button on the Standard toolbar.

⌐ **Note** ─────────────────

You cannot paste the data into a larger or smaller range than the original range. The source and destination ranges must contain the same number of rows and columns.

To insert new cells to make room for the copied data

1 Highlight the cell or range you want to copy.

2 Press and hold down the Ctrl and Shift keys (Ctrl+Shift), and then click and drag on the border edge of the selected range. As you move the mouse, the insert indicator shows where the cells will be inserted into the worksheet. Note that a vertical indicator shows that cells to the right will be moved aside to make room; a horizontal indicator shows that cells below will be moved down to make room.

3 Release the mouse button at the desired location. The copy will be inserted into the worksheet and existing information will move to make room for the inserted data.

To copy a text entry across several cells (fill)

1 Highlight the cell containing the text entry. (You can highlight several text cells if desired.)

2 Click and drag on the lower-right corner of the selected cell or range. This corner has a small box in it. The mouse pointer will change to a plus sign when you move to the correct location. Drag left, right, up, or down to copy the entry into adjacent cells.

3 Release the mouse when you finish.

Tip

If the data you copy using this method contains numeric values or a series, such as months, days, or dates, you will end up with a series of values based on the starting value.

To copy a numeric value down a column

1 Enter the first numeric value or formula into the first cell of the column.

2 Highlight the second cell in the column (directly under the first entry).

3 Press Shift+Ctrl+" (quotation mark) to duplicate the data in the selected cell.

4 Release the keys, and then press Enter to enter the value into the selected cell.

Tip

If the original cell contains a formula, the copied version of the cell will contain only the resulting value produced by the formula. To copy the entire formula, press Ctrl+' (apostrophe) rather than Shift+Ctrl+" (quotation mark).

To copy a column of data into a row (transpose data)

1 Highlight the range of data you want to copy and transpose.

2 Choose **E**dit **C**opy or press Ctrl+C. You also can click the Copy button on the Standard toolbar.

3 Highlight the first cell of the destination range. The copied data will begin at this location and fill cells across (to transpose a column into a row) or down (to transpose a row into a column).

4 Choose **E**dit Paste **S**pecial. The Paste Special dialog box appears.

5 Check the Transpose check box.

6 Choose OK.

See also *Moving Elements*.

To copy an object to another location on the sheet

1 Click the object to select it.

2 Press and hold down the Ctrl key, and then click and drag the object. As you drag, the copy will move with the mouse pointer.

3 Drag the object to the location you want and then release the mouse button.

To copy an object between pages, workbooks, or programs using the Clipboard

1 Click the object to select it.

2 Choose **E**dit Copy or press Ctrl+C. You also can click the Copy button on the Standard toolbar.

3 Move to the new sheet or workbook, or move into a different application by pressing Ctrl+Esc and selecting the application.

4 Select the location of the upper left corner of the object.

5 Choose **E**dit **P**aste or press Ctrl+V. You also can click the Paste button on the Standard toolbar.

To copy a formula across several cells in a column or row

1 Enter the formula you want into the first cell of the row or column.

2 Highlight the cell containing the formula you want to copy.

3 Click the lower right corner of the cell's border and drag to "stretch" the selection across the row or down the column. The mouse pointer changes to a plus sign when you move it to the right lower corner of the selection.

> ┌─ **Note** ─────────────────
>
> When you copy formulas using this procedure, the new formulas will adjust to reflect their respective rows or columns—a formula that adds the cells in column A, for example, will add the cells in column B when copied to the bottom of that column.

To copy a formula to non-adjacent cells using the Clipboard

1 Highlight the cell containing the formula you want to copy.

2 Choose **Edit Copy** or press Ctrl+C. You also can click the Copy button on the Standard toolbar.

3 Highlight the cell or range into which you want to copy the formula.

4 Choose **Edit Paste** or press Ctrl+V. You also can click the Paste button on the Standard toolbar.

To copy formulas without updating the references (absolute references)

1 Highlight the cell containing the formula you want.

2 Using the mouse, inside the formula bar, highlight the cell reference inside the formula you don't want adjusted when you copy the formula. This may be one of many references in the formula.

3 Press F4 to make the reference completely absolute. Excel places dollar signs between the row and column portions of the reference. If the reference was C5, for example, the new reference will be C5.

4 Repeat steps 2 and 3 to adjust any other references in the formula. Some references in the formula may remain relative while others are changed to absolute status.

5 Press Enter to save the changes to the formula.

6 Copy the formula into any other cells using any method described in this section. Note that the absolute cell references in the formula will not change when copied, but will reference the same cells.

Tip

You can make a cell reference partially absolute so that the row or column portion of the reference will adjust. This can be useful for certain types of copy procedures. Each time you press F4 while the cell reference is highlighted in the formula bar, a different combination of relativity is offered. A dollar sign preceding the row portion of the reference makes the row absolute; a dollar sign preceding the column portion makes the column absolute.

To copy cell notes to other cells

1 Highlight the cell containing the note you want to copy.

2 Choose **E**dit **C**opy or press Ctrl+C. You also can click the Copy button on the Standard toolbar.

3 Highlight the cell into which you want to copy the note.

4 Choose **E**dit Paste **S**pecial. The Paste Special dialog box appears.

5 Choose the **N**otes option button in the Paste area.

6 Choose OK.

To copy data from within a note into another note

1 Choose Insert Note. The Cell Note dialog box appears.

2 In the Notes in **S**heet list box, highlight the note containing the source data. The note should appear in the **T**ext Note box.

3 Drag the mouse to highlight the text you want.

4 Press Ctrl+C.

5 In the Notes in **S**heet list box, highlight the note into which the copied data is to appear.

6 Click inside the **T**ext Note box to choose a location for the copied data.

7 Press Ctrl+V.

To copy cell formats to other cells

1 Highlight the cell containing the format you want to copy.

2 Choose **E**dit **C**opy or press Ctrl+C. You also can click the Copy button on the Standard toolbar.

3 Highlight the cell or range into which you want to copy the format.

4 Choose **E**dit Paste **S**pecial. The Paste Special dialog box appears.

5 Choose the Formats option button in the Paste area.

Tip

You also can use the Format Painter button on the Standard toolbar. Highlight the range that contains the formats you want to copy. Click the Format Painter button on the Standard toolbar. The mouse pointer changes to a thick crosshair with a paint brush. Highlight the range you want to format.

6 Choose OK.

To use cell formats repeatedly as styles

1 Highlight the cell containing the formatting you want to use repeatedly.

2 Choose Format Style. The Style dialog box appears.

3 Click to remove the X from any of the Style Includes check boxes if you don't want the format to include that information.

4 Enter a new name into the Style Name drop-down list box. Typing a new name in this box does not remove or replace any existing styles.

5 Choose OK.

6 To apply the style to any other cell, highlight the cell, and then choose Format Style. The Style dialog box appears.

7 From the Style Name list box, select the name of the format (the name you created in step 4).

8 Choose OK.

Tip

Excel provides a Style button you can add to an existing or custom toolbar. This button is located in the Customize dialog box under Formatting. For more information about customizing toolbars, see *Toolbars*.

See also *Styles*.

Cross Tabulation

See *Pivot Tables*

Currency

See *Formatting*

Database Management

To facilitate management of data in the worksheet, you can organize the data as a *list*. Excel uses the list as simple database. You skip the chore of defining database fields and creating data entry screens simply by entering your list of data into the worksheet rows and columns, or by using the automatic data form. Each row of the list represents a single *record*. For example, a client's Name, Company, Street, City, State, Zip Code, Phone Number, and Date Contacted could be listed across a row of the list; this row of data is a record. Each item in the record occupies one cell, and is called a *field*. Name is a field, Company is a field, and so forth. In a list, the names of the fields are entered in the first row, thus each field name serves as a column heading to identify the kind of data in that column. Name is column A, Company is column B, and so on.

As you enter a series of rows, each row being another client's information, you are adding to the database list. Excel has automatic features to allow you to *sort* the data by the contents of any field, for example alphabetically by name, or sorted numerically in ZIP code order. *Filtering* allows you to select only certain records for reporting or processing, based on selection criteria. For example, you could filter to select only the clients from the State of Ohio whose Date Contacted was more than three months ago. After you create a list by entering field names across a row, you can use Excel's data form to add, delete, find, or edit records.

Setting Up a Database List

Creating the Excel database list is easy, but there are a few setup guidelines that will make management of the list more efficient. In order to take full advantage of features of the lists, such as filtering, set up only one list on a worksheet. A list may be as large as the worksheet: 16,384 rows by 256 columns, however, it does not need exclusive use of the worksheet. You may include charts and other data on the same worksheet as the list. It is recommended that at least one blank row and column surround the list, to separate it from other data on the worksheet. This will help Excel to select the list automatically for sorting, filtering, and subtotaling.

Entering Column Headings

The column headings, or labels, are the first row of the list. Enter text to represent a unique field name for each column, one label per cell. All the field names must be in a single row. You can use the Format Cells command to choose various formatting features for the column labels, to make them look different than the data in the list: font, border, pattern, format, and alignment.

Caution!

Do not put a row of dashed lines or blanks in the row below the field names; use cell borders if you want to create a line.

Field names can be up to 255 characters in length, but shorter names are easier to see in the cells. If the field name you want to use is wider than the data in the column, you can turn on word wrap to "stack" the heading in the cell. This will keep the headings in the required single row, yet allow the field name to be more descriptive.

To turn on word wrap

1 Highlight the cell or range containing labels you want to wrap.

2 Choose Format Cells or press Ctrl+1 to display the Format Cells dialog box.

3 Click the Alignment tab.

4 Click the Wrap Text check box.

5 Choose OK. The row height is automatically adjusted. You can make further adjustments to row height or column width to change the appearance of the column headings.

Naming the Database List

Although assigning a name to the list is optional, names are useful in quickly moving between lists. If you have only one list in the worksheet, as recommended, the commands on the Data menu will find this list. If you assign the name Database to your list, the commands on the Data menu will default to the list named Database. You may assign the name of the list to a single cell or to the range.

To name the database list

1 Highlight a cell in the field names row or highlight the entire range of field names and data in the list.

2 Choose Insert Name Define to display the Define Name dialog box.

3 In the Names in Workbook list box, enter a descriptive name. Begin with a letter and do not use spaces.

4 Click the Refers to text box to select a different cell or range.

5 Choose the Add button to add the new name to the Names in Workbook list box.

6 Choose OK.

Now that the list is named you can easily select it. Choose **E**dit **G**o To or press F5, and then in the Go To dialog box choose the name from the **G**o To list box and choose OK.

Tip

You can select the database list by clicking its name from the Name drop-down list box at the left end of the formula bar. You also can define a list name by selecting the range, and then entering the name in the Name drop-down list box.

Adding Records

There are two common methods of adding data to the list: entering directly in the cells of the worksheet, or using the data form that Excel creates for the list.

Type data directly into the worksheet in the usual way. Tab from cell to cell across the row, entering the type of data you defined for each field in the column heading. If you named the list as a range, you must insert new rows between existing rows of the list to keep the new data in the defined range. The best way to insert the new rows is to highlight cells in the middle of a list and insert new cells, not entire worksheet rows, to preserve the formatting for each column and not disturb the data to the right or left outside the list.

To insert new rows

1 Highlight the cells from one side of the list to the other, including as many rows as records you want to add. To make room for three records, for example, highlight three rows of list cells.

2 Choose **I**nsert **C**ells or press Ctrl+Shift++ (plus), or with the mouse pointer in the selected range, right-click and choose Insert from the shortcut menu. The Insert dialog box appears.

3 Click the Shift Cells **D**own option button.

4 Choose OK.

To enter records with the data form

1 Highlight a cell within the list, or choose a named list by choosing **E**dit **G**o To or pressing F5. Then choose the name from the **G**o to list box in the Go To dialog box and choose OK.

2 Choose **D**ata Form. The data form dialog box appears, with the name of the worksheet in the title bar. Along the left side of the data form are the fields, with names from the column labels in the worksheet list.

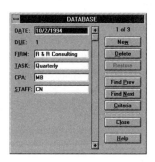

3 To enter a new record, choose the Ne**w** button.

4 Type data in the field text boxes (also called *edit boxes*). Fields which contain calculated results appear, but cannot be edited. Be sure to use the Tab key, not the Enter key, to move between fields.

5 Press Enter to add the record to the list.

6 To enter additional records, repeat steps 3 through 5.

7 Choose the Close button to close the form and return to the worksheet.

The records added with the data form are placed below the last row of the list. The fields in the new record are formatted like the previous record. The data form will not allow you to add new records if there are not enough blank cells below the current list range. You will receive the warning `Cannot extend database when there is no more room to expand downward.`

Sorting the Database

You use the Sort command to arrange the rows of the database list in a particular order, based on the contents of the fields, or columns. Excel uses the following order for an ascending sort: numbers, text and text that includes numbers, logical values, error values, and blanks. Sorting in descending order reverses the order, except for blanks, which are always sorted last.

Tip

If you want to sort a column that contains both numbers and numbers that contain text characters, for example: 1, 1A, 2, 2A, format them all as text so they will sort together. Otherwise, the numbers will sort first: 1, 2, 1A, 2A. To format the numbers as text, precede the number with an apostrophe: '1.

To sort the database

1 Highlight the range you want to sort. If the range you want to sort is surrounded by blank cells, you can click a cell in the range.

Note

Be sure the full width of the list is selected. If you neglect to include some columns, they will not be sorted with the other data, resulting in scrambled records. If you sort by columns, the same problem can occur if you do not select the full column height. If this happens, or for any other reason you do not like the results of the sort, you can undo the sort immediately by choosing **Edit Undo Sort**, pressing Ctrl+Z, or clicking the Undo button on the Standard toolbar.

---

2 Choose **Data Sort** to display the Sort dialog box.

3 If the list has text field names in the top row, choose the Header **R**ow option button in the My List Has area. This ensures that the field names will not be sorted in with the data. If your list or database does not have field names, choose the No Header Ro**w** option button.

4 Click the **S**ort By drop-down list box and choose the field name of the first column by which you want to sort. If your data does not have labels in a header row, then select the first cell at the top of the column by which you want to sort.

5 Choose the sort order by clicking the **A**scending or **D**escending option buttons in the **S**ort By area.

Note

Ascending order puts the lowest number, the beginning of the alphabet, or the earliest date first in the list. Descending order starts with the highest number, the end of the alphabet, or the latest date.

---

6 Choose the secondary sort field in the **T**hen By drop-down list box. Choose the Ascending or Descending option button. The second sort field is only used if there is duplicate data in the first sort field.

7 Choose the tertiary sort field in the Then **B**y drop-down list box. Choose the Ascending or Descending option button. The third sort field is only used if there is duplicate data in the first and second sort field.

8 Choose OK.

Tip

Use the Sort Ascending and Sort Descending buttons on the Standard toolbar if you only need to sort by one field (column). Excel will sort the entire list, except column labels. These buttons use the custom sort options, as described in the next section.

To sort the database using a custom sort order

1 Highlight the range you want to sort. If the range you want to sort is surrounded by blank cells, you can click a cell in the range.

2 Choose **D**ata **S**ort to display the Sort dialog box.

3 Choose the **O**ptions button to display the Sort Options dialog box.

4 If the primary sort is by names of the months or names of the days of the week, select the appropriate entry in the **F**irst Key Sort Order drop-down list box. Otherwise leave the Normal option selected.

5 Click the **C**ase Sensitive check box if you want a sort dependent on upper- and lowercase.

6 To sort a list from left to right order rather than top to bottom order, click the Sort **L**eft to Right option button in the Orientation area. The default orientation is Sort **T**op to Bottom.

7 Choose OK to return to the Sort dialog box.

8 Choose a row name in the **S**ort By drop-down text box.

9 Choose other options in the Sort dialog box, as described in previous section. Note that the My List Has area is unavailable because the rows do not have labels.

10 Choose OK.

Filtering a List Using AutoFilter

Filtering enables you to work with a subset of your data without moving or sorting it. The AutoFilter command attaches drop-down arrows to column labels. Selecting an item from a drop-down list hides all rows except rows that contain the selected value. You then can perform editing and formatting commands on the cells that are visible.

You can filter only one list at a time on a worksheet. Choose **Data Filter**. If there is a check mark next to the AutoFilter command, select the AutoFilter command to turn it off before selecting another list.

Note

Data stored to the left or right of the list may be hidden when you filter the list. If other data shares the worksheet with the list, store it in rows above or below the list area.

To use AutoFilter on a list

1 Select a cell within the list.

2 Choose **Data Filter AutoFilter**. Drop-down arrows appear next to each column label in the list.

3 Click the drop-down list for the column that contains data you want to display, or highlight the column label and press Alt+↓. The drop-down list box shows all of the unique values for that column.

4 Select the criterion you want to display from the following options:

(All)	Displays all records in this field.
(Custom...)	Displays the Custom AutoFilter dialog box enabling you to create AND or OR criteria.

Exact values   Displays only records with this exact value in this field.

(Blanks)   Displays all records with blanks in this field.

(NonBlanks)   Displays all records with a value other than blanks in this field.

5 Complete the Custom AutoFilter dialog box if you selected the (Custom...) option. If you selected one of the other options, you immediately see the results of your filter.

6 Repeat steps 3 through 5 to further filter the data displayed. You may want to select the (All) option on the field you just filtered to redisplay those hidden rows before filtering others.

7 To display all records and remove the criteria from all AutoFilters, choose **D**ata **F**ilter **S**how All.

8 To discontinue AutoFilter for this list, choose **D**ata **F**ilter Auto**F**ilter. The check mark is removed from the AutoFilter command on the menu, and the drop-down arrows disappear from the column labels.

Filtering a List Using Custom Criteria

By using the Custom AutoFilter dialog box, you can take AutoFilter beyond finding exact matches, to specifying near matches or many AND and OR conditions.

To use Custom AutoFilter

1 Start AutoFilter as described in the previous section. Choose (Custom...) from the drop-down list box that is attached to column label for which you want to specify criteria. The Custom AutoFilter dialog box appears. The name of the field (column label) you selected is shown in the Show Rows Where area.

2 To enter comparative criteria, choose a comparison operator from the first drop-down list box, and then type or select the value from the drop-down list to its right. Following is the meaning of the comparison operators in the drop-down list box:

Operator	Meaning
=	Equal to
>	Greater than
<	Less than
>=	Greater than or equal to
<=	Less than or equal to
<>	Not equal to

3 If you have a second comparison, choose the And or Or option button, and then select the second comparison operator and the second comparison value from their drop-down list boxes. Following is an example of a completed comparison:

Show Rows Where Date >= 11/6/94 And <= 12/25/94

This comparison would select dates in the range between and including the two dates entered.

4 Choose OK. If you don't like the results, you can choose the (All) option from the column's drop-down list box to bring back the hidden rows.

Tip

Find blank fields by using the = comparison operator followed by nothing. Find filled fields by using the not equal to operator, <>, followed by nothing.

Searching the Database

Excel's data form can be used to find and edit records that satisfy simple or multiple comparisons. You can use the data form to browse the list one record at a time. You also can use the scroll bar to "zip ahead" to a different place in the list.

To browse in the data form

1 Highlight a cell within the list or choose a named list by choosing **E**dit **G**o To or pressing F5. Then select the name from the **G**o to list box in the Go To dialog box and then choose OK.

2 Choose **D**ata F**o**rm. The data form dialog box appears with the name of the worksheet in the title bar. On the left side of the data form are the fields, with names from the column labels in the worksheet list.

3 To display records beginning with the first one in the list, choose the Find **N**ext button. As you repeatedly click the Find **N**ext button, the succeeding records appear, and the record number in the upper right corner of the dialog box increments. Use Find **P**rev to back up to the previous record. If criteria are already selected, Find **N**ext and Find **P**rev go to the next and previous record meeting the criteria. Pressing the up- and down-arrows on the keyboard also will move to the next or previous record.

4 The scroll bar is useful for quickly moving ahead or back in the records. Drag the scroll box to the bottom of the scroll bar to view the last record, or to the top of the scroll bar to view the first record. Click below the scroll box to move forward 10 records, or above the scroll bar to move back 10 records. Click the down scroll arrow to move to the same field in the next record; the up scroll arrow takes you to the same field in the previous record.

5 When finished browsing, choose the C**l**ose button to close the form and return to the worksheet.

To use the data form to find records

1 Select a cell within the list or select a named list by choosing **Edit Go** To or pressing F5. Then select the name from the **Go** to list box in the Go To dialog box and then choose OK.

2 Choose **Data Form**. The data form dialog box appears with the name of the worksheet in the title bar.

3 Select the **Criteria** button. The data form changes slightly, making the **Clear** and **Form** buttons available.

4 Highlight the text box next to the field in which you want to enter a criterion. Type the criterion.

5 Click another box or press Tab for the next box, Shift+Tab for the previous box, or press the Alt+key combination for a particular field, if it has one; enter other criteria as desired.

While using the criteria form, you can choose the **Clear** button to remove the existing criteria from the search boxes or choose the **Form** button to return to the data form.

Note

Enter criteria in one or more field text boxes in the criteria dialog box. Use comparison operators: = > < >= <= <> (as described in the *Filtering* section) along with text, to create an expression such as >5000. You also can enter text to search for an exact match, or include the wildcard characters: ? and *, where ? is replaced by a single character and * is replaced by multiple characters. The criteria in the data form have an AND relationship.

6 Choose Find **N**ext or Find **P**rev to initiate the search, and then to move from the current record to the next or previous record that meets the entered search criteria.

7 Choose the C**l**ose button to close the data form and return to the worksheet.

To edit data using the data form

1 Highlight a cell within the list or select a named list by choosing **E**dit **G**o To or pressing F5. Select the name from the **G**o to list box in the Go To dialog box and then choose OK.

2 Choose **D**ata **F**orm. The data form dialog box appears, with the name of the worksheet in the title bar.

3 Find the record you want to edit. Use the **C**riteria button as described in the previous section, or scroll through the list using the scroll bar.

4 If you have found the record you want to edit, click the text box next to the field you want to change. Edit the data. If you make changes and want to undo your changes before you have moved to the next record, then choose the **R**estore button.

5 Press Enter to save the changes.

6 Repeat steps 3 through 5 until you have found and edited the records you want.

7 Choose the C**l**ose button to close the data form and return to the worksheet.

Extracting and Deleting Data from the Database

You may want to work with a subset of your data at times, for example, to extract a partial list of data to give to someone who does not need to have access to the entire database list. Or, perhaps you want a report using a filtered view of the data, uncluttered by extraneous data. You can filter your data and move it elsewhere: to another worksheet, workbook, or external application. Occasionally, you may want to delete unwanted records from the list. This can be accomplished by filtering or other methods described in this section.

There are two ways in which you can extract data to copy to another worksheet. The first method uses the AutoFilter tool to copy and paste a limited amount of data. The second method uses the Advanced Filter to copy larger amounts of data, or data requiring complex criteria, to another location.

To copy a list with AutoFilter

1 Use the **D**ata Filter AutoFilter command to filter the list, as explained in the earlier section, "Filtering a list using AutoFilter."

2 Highlight the data and choose **E**dit **C**opy. The Copy command copies only the data shown by the filter.

> ## ┌─ Shortcut ─────────────────────
> Press Ctrl+C or click the Copy button on the Standard toolbar.

3 Click the sheet tab of the sheet which you want to contain the data.

4 Highlight the cell that will be the top left corner of the new list.

5 Choose **E**dit **P**aste. The data is now moved to this new location.

> ## ┌─ Shortcut ─────────────────────
> Press Ctrl+V or click the Paste button on the Standard toolbar.

To copy to the same sheet with an Advanced Filter

Use the Advanced Filter method of copying data if the criteria you need to use is too complex for the AutoFilter or if you need to restrict the number of rows or columns copied.

1 Create field names (column labels) for the Copy to range (the area of the worksheet that will receive the extracted data) by copying the single row of field names from the column headings at the top of the list.

The field names must be exactly the same as the field names at the top of the list, yet a subset of field names is allowed. Arrange the field names in the order you want the columns of data to appear.

2 Enter the filter criteria in the criteria range.

The *criteria range* is the range on the worksheet where selection criteria are entered for Advanced Filter operations. The range consists of a row of field names with cells below to enter the comparison operators and operands.

3 Highlight a cell in the database list.

4 Choose **D**ata **F**ilter **A**dvanced Filter to display the Advanced Filter dialog box.

5 In the Action area, choose the C**o**py to Another Location option button.

6 Click the **L**ist Range text box. If the correct range is not already displayed, type in the range name or drag across the worksheet area to define the list range.

7 Select the **C**riteria Range text box and type in the range name or drag across the worksheet area to highlight the predefined (see step 2) criteria range.

8 Select the Copy **t**o text box and type in the range name or drag across the worksheet area defining the area to receive the filtered copy. The following figure shows an example of an Advanced Filter.

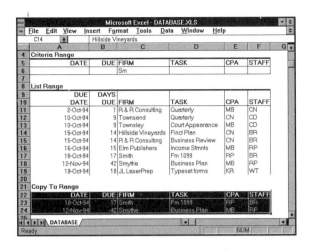

Tip

Use the **I**nsert **N**ame **D**efine command to
define a name for the Copy to range, then
use the name in the Copy **t**o text box. If you
assign the name *Extract* to the Copy to
range, Excel will recognize it and display its
cell references in the Copy **t**o text box.

For the Copy to range, click the upper left corner
cell or select only the field names at the top of the
predefined range (see step 1) for an unlimited length
list. Or select the field names and a limited area
below the field names to confine the list to the cells
available in this range. Excel will leave out data that
does not fit and give a warning message.

9 If you want to avoid duplicate records, click the
Unique **R**ecords Only check box.

10 Choose OK.

**To copy filtered data between worksheets
or workbooks**

1 Open the workbooks containing the Criteria, List,
and Copy to range.

2 Activate the worksheet containing the Copy to
range.

3 Highlight a blank cell that is not touching filled cells.
This will inhibit Excel from attempting to define the
database range.

4 Choose Data Filter Advanced Filter to display the
Advanced Filter dialog box.

5 In the Action area, select the Copy to Another Location option button.

6 Click the List Range text box, and then activate the
worksheet containing the list. (Click it or select it
from the Window menu.) Drag across the database
range or click the cell in the sheet and edit the reference to include the name of the list.

7 Click the Criteria Range text box and enter a range
by activating the sheet containing the criteria range
and dragging across that range.

8 Select the Copy to range box and enter the copy to
range from the original worksheet that was active in
step 2.

9 Click the Unique Records Only check box if you
want to remove duplicates.

10 Choose OK.

Deleting Records

Deleting records, rows of the database list, can be
accomplished directly in the worksheet, or by filtering
the list or by using the data form.

You can use apply a filter to show only the records you want to delete, then choose the **E**dit **D**elete command to delete the filtered records. However, if you have only a few records to delete, or if the records are difficult to describe with criteria, you may want to delete them manually. Use **D**ata **F**orm to find the records and then select the **D**elete button on the form to delete the current record.

If you need to delete a record you have found with the data form, choose the **D**elete button on the form. An alert message will warn that you are about to permanently delete the current record. Choose OK to complete the deletion, or click Cancel to avoid deleting the record. Keep in mind that deleted records cannot be recovered.

To delete a record directly in the list

1 Highlight a record in the list by dragging on the entire row you want to delete. Highlight more than one row to delete multiple records.

Do not miss a single column, or that column's data will remain stationary when the cells shift to fill in for the delete. Do not highlight the entire worksheet row by clicking in the row header unless you have no other data next to the list in the worksheet.

2 Choose **E**dit **D**elete or click the right mouse button within the selected row or rows and choose Delete from the shortcut menu. The Delete dialog box appears.

3 Select the Shift Cells **U**p option button. (This button probably is already selected.)

4 Choose OK. The records you selected for deletion are gone and the list has moved up to fill the gap.

┌─ **Note** ────────────────────────────────

If you want to restore the records you just deleted, you must use the **E**dit **U**ndo command or press Ctrl+Z immediately. You cannot similarly undo a Delete executed within the data form.

└──

Date Math

In Excel, dates are actually numeric values that have been formatted to appear as dates. The numeric value represents the number of days and "day portions" that have elapsed since January 1, 1900. Hence, the date January 2, 1900 is represented by the value 2. Because dates are numbers, you can make calculations with them—a function known as date math.

> ┌ **Tip** ──────────────────────
>
> Days are measured in decimal values. Excel measures each elapsed decimal fraction of a date. The number 2.2, for example, represents that two and two-tenths days have elapsed since 1/1/1900. This would be the date 1/2/1900 and the time of approximately 4:48a.m.

To calculate the difference between two dates in days or weeks

1 Enter the first date into cell A1 (or any other cell).

2 Enter the second date into cell A2 (or any other cell).

3 Enter the formula =**A1-A2** into cell A3 (or any other cell) to get the difference between the first and second dates. Enter the formula =**A2-A1** to calculate the difference between the second and first dates. These formulas calculate the number of days elapsed between the two dates. Use the formulas =**(A1-A2)/7** or =**(A2-A1)/7** to calculate the difference in weeks.

To add days or weeks to a date

1 Enter a date into cell A1 (or any other cell).

2 Enter the formula **=A1+120** into cell A2 (or any other
cell) to add 120 days to the date. Change the number 120 to any other number or use a reference to a
cell containing the desired number. To add weeks to
a date, simply multiply the number of weeks by 7 to
get the number of days, as in =A1+(5*7) to add 5
weeks to the date. Change the five to any other
number.

To add months to a date

1 Type a date into cell A1 (or any other cell).

2 Enter the formula

=DATE(YEAR(A1),MONTH(A1)+1,DAY(A1))

into cell A2 Change the value +1 to +2 to add
two months, and so on.

To determine the last day of the month

1 Type a date into cell A1 (or any other cell).

2 Enter the formula

=DATE(YEAR(A1),MONTH(A1)+1,1)-1

into cell A2 The result is a date representing
the last day of the month found in cell A1.

Decimal Places

Any numeric value in Excel can be displayed with up to
16 decimal places (including the decimal point). You can
control the number of decimal places displayed with a
number by formatting the number. Formatting the
number does not actually change the value—it merely
displays the value with more or fewer decimal places.
For example, the number 3.49834 may be displayed as
3.5, but the entire number is used for calculations.
However, if you actually round the value, Excel uses the
rounded value for calculations.

To establish a fixed number of decimal places for cell formats

1 Highlight the cell or range you want to format with a
fixed number of decimal places.

2 [+.0/.00] [.00/+.0] Click the Increase Decimal button on the Formatting toolbar to add a decimal point to the selected values. Continue to click until you add as many decimals as you want. Click the Decrease Decimal button to remove decimal values.

To round a number to a specific number of decimal places

1 Highlight the cell containing the value you want to round.

2 Edit the data in the formula bar to read =ROUND(data,2). The word data represents the existing information in the cell, whether a value or formula. Change the 2 to any number of decimal places you want to use. If the cell contains the formula =C5*G1, for example, you would change it to =ROUND(C5*G1,1) to round the value to one decimal place.

To remove decimal values from numbers

1 Highlight the cell containing the value for which you want the integer portion.

2 Edit the data in the formula bar to read =INT(data). The word data represents the existing information in the cell, whether a value or formula. If the cell contains the formula =C5*G1, for example, you would change it to =INT(C5*G1).

To remove the integer portion of a number

1 Highlight the cell containing the value for which you want the integer portion.

2 Edit the data in the formula bar to read =(data)-INT(data). The word data represents the existing information in the cell, whether a value or formula. If the cell contained the formula =C5*G1, for example, you would change it to =(C5*G1)-INT(C5*G1).

To set decimal places for all numeric values on the workbook

1 Choose **T**ools **O**ptions. The Options dialog box appears.

2 Click the Edit tab.

3 Check the Fixed Decimal Places check box.

4 Change the number of decimal places in the spin box to the desired number of places for the workbook.

5 Choose OK. You now can enter numbers without typing the decimal point. This does not affect existing data.

To align numbers by their decimal points

1 Highlight the cells containing the numbers you want to align.

2 Choose Format Cells or press Ctrl+1. The Format Cells dialog box appears.

3 Click the Number tab.

4 Click the Custom category in the Category list box.

5 Press Tab to move to the Code text box. Type the new code ??.???? in the text box, replacing the previous entry.

6 Choose OK.

Deleting

Although deleting data is a simple, straight-forward task, there are a few options with which you should be familiar. You can clear the data from cells in the worksheet, or you can delete the cells themselves. If you delete cells from the worksheet, the remaining cells shift to fill the space left by the deleted cells.

To delete the contents of a cell or range

1 Highlight the cell or range you want to erase.

2 Press the Delete key.

> ┌ **Note** ──────────────────────
>
> If you delete values used in formulas
> throughout the worksheet, those formulas
> will return errors.

To erase data without disturbing the underlying cell formats

1 Highlight the cell or range whose data you want to remove.

2 Choose Edit Clear Contents. This removes the data from the cell or range without removing the formatting.

> ┌ **Tip** ──────────────────────
>
> To remove the formatting of a cell without
> removing the actual data, use the Edit Clear
> Formats command.

To delete entire rows or columns

1 Highlight the row(s) and/or column(s) you want to remove by clicking the row number or column letter.

2 Choose Edit Delete. The data in the row or column is deleted. The other rows or columns move up or over, respectively.

To delete cells or ranges

1 Highlight the cell or range you want to delete.

2 Choose Edit Delete. The Delete dialog box appears.

3 Choose the Shift Cells Up option button to make the remaining cells move up to fill the space left by the deleted cells. Choose the Shift Cells Left option button to fill the space from the cell to the right of the selection.

4 Choose OK.

To delete objects

1 Click the object to select it.

2 Press the Delete key to remove the object.

To delete worksheets

1 Activate the worksheet you want to remove.

2 Choose **E**dit Delete Sheet. The Microsoft Excel dialog box warns you that the selected sheets will be permanently deleted.

3 Choose OK to continue with the operation. Choose Cancel to avoid deleting the worksheet.

Drawing

Excel enables you to add graphics to your worksheets by drawing objects right inside Excel. A host of drawing buttons enable you to create ovals, rectangles, polygons and freehand lines. By combining these objects, you can create all kinds of images. Drawn objects can enhance your worksheet reports, add annotation elements to your charts and graphs, and generally spruce-up your worksheets. The following topics provide the details.

Drawing Objects and Shapes

To draw objects and shapes in Excel, you must first access the Drawing toolbar. Using the various buttons on this toolbar, you can draw basic shapes, change the colors and borders of those shapes, and generally manipulate your drawn images. You can draw most shapes with a simple click-and-drag motion of the mouse.

To displaying the Drawing toolbar

1 Choose **V**iew **T**oolbars command. The toolbars dialog box appears.

2 In the Toolbars list box, click the Drawing toolbar check box.

3 Choose OK.

⌐ Shortcut ─────────────────────

 You can quickly show and hide the Drawing
toolbar by clicking the Drawing button on
the Standard toolbar.

To draw lines, boxes, ovals, and arcs

1 With the Drawing toolbar on-screen, click the button
you want to select. Click the Rectangle tool to draw
a rectangle, for example.

⌐ Note ─────────────────────

Excel provides two versions of some of the
drawing buttons; one creates an empty
object and the other creates an object filled
with a color. You can always fill the empty
object later if desired.

---

2 Click the worksheet, and then drag the mouse to
create the desired size for the object. When you
release the mouse button, the object will fill the
area you "drew" onto the screen. The following
figure shows different lines, rectangles, ovals,
and arcs you can draw.

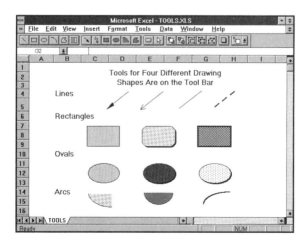

Tip

If you hold the Shift key down as you draw an oval or rectangle, Excel creates a perfect circle or square. If you press Shift while drawing an arc, Excel creates a perfect semicircle. Press Shift while drawing a line and you get a perfectly horizontal, vertical, or 45-degree diagonal line. If you hold down the Alt key as you draw objects, the object will fit into the cell grid. If you press Alt as you draw a rectangle, for example, the rectangle will match the size and shape of the cells beneath it.

To draw polygons and freeform shapes

1 Click the Freeform or Filled Freeform buttons on the Drawing toolbar.

2 Click the worksheet to begin the freeform drawing, and then drag the mouse to draw form lines.

3 To draw a straight line as one side of the shape, release the mouse button to end the current line, and then click elsewhere to draw a straight line between the ending point and the mouse position.

4 Return to the starting point of the shape and click the mouse to close the shape. You also can end the shape without closing the object by double-clicking wherever you want to end the line.

To draw freehand lines

1 Click the Freehand button on the Drawing toolbar.

2 Click the worksheet to begin the freehand drawing, and then drag the mouse to draw freehand lines. End the drawing by releasing the mouse button.

To draw a text box and enter text

1 Click the Text Box button on the Drawing toolbar.

2 Click and drag on the worksheet to draw a text box of any size. When you release the mouse, the box will appear with the cursor flashing inside it.

3 Type the text you want inside the box.

Arranging Objects

Once you have drawn objects on the sheet, you can move them around to make them work together. Because Excel's drawing capabilities are object-oriented, each object appears on an invisible "layer" above the worksheet. You may want to change how the objects overlap each other. You also can combine objects into groups; a group behaves as a single object.

To move an object around the page

1 Click the object and hold down the mouse button.

2 Drag the object to a new location. Release the mouse button when you are finished.

Tip

If you have to move an object a large distance within a worksheet or between two worksheet pages, first choose **E**dit **C**ut, press Ctrl+X, or click the Cut button on the Standard toolbar to remove the object from its original location. Move to the new location, and then choose **E**dit **P**aste, press Ctrl+V, or click the Paste button on the Standard toolbar to place the object into the new position.

To bring an object to the front or back of others

1 Click the object once to select it.

2 Click the Bring To Front button on the Drawing toolbar to bring the object to the front. Click the Send To Back button to move it behind others. You may need to manipulate several objects in a specific order to get the arrangement you want.

To combine objects into a group

1 Click the first object in the group.

2 Hold down the Shift key and click all other objects in the group. All the objects should remain selected.

3 Click the Group Objects button on the Drawing toolbar. The grouped object can be copied or moved as a single group.

4 To return a grouped object to its original, independent elements, highlight the group, and then click the Ungroup Objects button on the Drawing toolbar.

Tip

You can place an object group into another grouped object. If you want to ungroup the objects, you must ungroup in the reverse order in which you grouped the objects.

To copy objects

1 Press and hold down the Ctrl key.

2 Click and drag the desired object. As you drag, a copy of the object moves with the mouse.

Tip

To copy an object between worksheets, use the **Edit C**opy and **Edit P**aste commands. You also can use the Ctrl+C and Ctrl+V keyboard shortcuts, or the Copy and Paste buttons on the Standard toolbar.

Borders and Fill Patterns

You can change the border of an object, making it thick or thin, red or blue. You also can remove the border entirely. Likewise, you can change the color and pattern of the objects interior.

To change the color of an object

1 Click the object to select it.

2 Click the down arrow to the right of the Color button on the Formatting toolbar. Choose a color from the palette.

To change the fill pattern of an object

1 Click the object to select it.

2 Click the Pattern button on the Drawing toolbar and choose a pattern. Patterns appear in the top three rows of the tear-off palette.

3 Click the Pattern button again to select a color for the chosen pattern.

To change the border style of an object

1 Double-click the object to display the Format Object dialog box.

2 Click the Patterns tab at the top of the dialog box.

3 Choose options from the Border area. To choose a border Style, Color, and Weight, click each drop down arrow, and then click the option you want. You also can add a drop-shadow by clicking the Shadow check box.

4 Choose OK.

To make an object transparent

1 Click the object to select it.

2 Click the down arrow to the right of the Color button on the Formatting toolbar. Choose the None color from the palette.

To change the shape of an arrow

1 Double-click the arrow to display the Format Object dialog box.

2 Click the Patterns tab at the top of the dialog box.

3 Choose options from the Arrowhead area. To choose a different **S**tyle, **W**idth, and **L**ength of arrow head, click each drop-down arrow, and then click the option you want. You also can change the arrow's line by using the Line options.

4 Choose OK.

Editing Groups of Worksheets

Excel enables you to perform operations to groups of worksheets at the same time. By forming a worksheet group, you can save much formatting, data entry, and editing time by applying the same operations to the entire group at once. This especially is useful for a set of worksheets that share a common look and feel, and perhaps common formulas and worksheet headings. You can form a group at any time to perform group operations, and then return the worksheets to normal when finished. When the group is formed, all your editing, data entry, and formatting actions are performed to all worksheets in the group.

To form a group

1 Click the sheet tab of the first worksheet in the group, activating that worksheet.

2 Hold down the Ctrl key and click all other sheet tabs you want to add to the group. If the sheets are sequential, hold down the Shift key and click the last sheet tab in the group.

3 Activate any of the group sheets by clicking its sheet tab.

Tip

To return grouped pages to normal, hold down the Shift key and click the active sheet tab. This removes the group status from other sheets. Alternatively, you can click any sheet that is not in the group.

Entering Data

Excel accepts several types of data: text, numbers, dates, and formulas. (See *Formulas* for information on entering formulas.) Typing the information is as easy as selecting the cell and typing away.

To enter numbers

1 Highlight the cell into which you want to enter a number.

2 Type the number. To type a negative number, precede the number with a minus sign or enclose the number in parentheses. You can type commas and a period (to indicate decimal places).

Note

By default, numbers are right-aligned and appear in the General number format. You can change the format. See *Formatting*.

Tip

To enter a number or formula as text, type an apostrophe and then type the entry.

To enter text

1 Highlight the cell you want.

2 Type the text.

Note

By default, text entries are left-aligned. You can change the alignment, font, and other aspects of a cell. See *Formatting*.

To enter dates or times

1 Highlight the cell you want.

2 Type the date or time. You can use either hyphens or slashes to separate the dates.

Tip

To enter the current date, press Ctrl+; (semicolon). To enter the current time, press Ctrl+Shift+: (colon).

To move the selection after you press Enter

1 Choose **T**ools **O**ptions. The Option dialog box appears.

2 Click the Edit tab.

3 Check or uncheck the **M**ove Selection after Enter check box. When the option is checked and you press Enter, Excel moves to the cell in the next row.

Exiting Excel

Microsoft Windows applications can open multiple document windows. Excel for Windows enables you to close individual workbook windows or to exit Excel entirely, closing all open windows.

To exit Excel

1 Choose **F**ile E**x**it or press Alt+F4. If you have saved all changes in active workbook files, Excel closes. If you have not saved all changes to active files, a confirmation box appears.

2 If the Save confirmation box appears, choose **Y**es to save the current workbook file before exiting; choose **N**o to exit without saving the file; choose Cancel or press Esc to cancel the E**x**it command and return to Excel. If you have multiple Workbook windows open, Excel will confirm the save before closing each Workbook that has been changed.

> **Tip**
>
> To quit Excel and return to the Program Manager, you also can double-click the Excel Control menu box. If the Save confirmation box appears, make your selection as outlined in step 2.

Files and File Management

File management is simply the act of saving and using workbook files in Excel. Excel's File menu has several commands that perform file management functions, such as saving files, opening existing files, and starting new files. The following sections provide details.

Opening

You can open a new workbook file at any time. Plus, you can open files you previously saved—so that you can work on them again. In Excel, you can work with several workbooks at once by simply opening all the files in one session. You can flip among workbook files in Excel by using the **W**indow menu. Following are some file opening tasks.

Note

The New Workbook button on the Standard toolbar opens a workbook based on the default template. Use the File New command to select a template. See *Templates*.

To start a new workbook file

1 Choose File New.

Shortcut

Press Ctrl+N or click the New Workbook button on the Standard toolbar.

2 If the New dialog box appears, double-click Work-book in the New list box. If no template exists in the XLSTART subdirectory, Excel skips the New dialog box and opens a new workbook based on the default template.

To open an existing workbook

1 Choose File Open.

Shortcut

Press Ctrl+O or click the Open button on the Standard toolbar.

2 From the Directories list box, choose the directory in which the file you want appears. Excel displays the default directory in this list automatically, but you can select any other directory on any disk by double-clicking the directory folders that appear. To view the folders (directories) inside the root directory, double-click the root directory, and then double-click one of those directories to view directories further down the path.

> **Note**
>
> You can change drives by choosing the drive you want from the Drives drop-down list box.

3 After you select the directory you want in the **Direc-**tories list box, the files inside that directory appear ın the File **N**ame list box Double-click the name of the file in that list to open it. You can view files of different types by choosing the file type from the List Files of **T**ype drop-down list box. See also *Converting.*

> **Tip**
>
> Excel stores the names and directory paths of the last four files you used. You can re-turn to any of these files by selecting the appropriate pathname from the bottom of the **F**ile menu (above the **E**xit command).

To find a file

1 Choose **F**ile **F**ind File. The Find File dialog box ap-pears. Choose the **S**earch button to display the Search dialog box.

2 Type the directory you want in the **L**ocation drop-down list box or choose from the directories offered in the list. This is the directory in which the Find feature will look for the files you specify.

3 Click to place a check mark into the Include Su**b**directories check box if you want to search for files inside the subdirectories of the directory you specified in step 2. Otherwise, the Find feature will look only in the directory you specified.

4 Choose a file type from the File **N**ame drop-down list box or enter a file specification of your own. This entry determines the files for which you are looking. Type **BUD*.XLS**, for example, to find all worksheet files that begin with BUD.

5 To save this search criteria for future searches, click the Save Search As button and enter a name for the search settings. You then can choose this name from the Saved Searches drop-down list box the next time you want to use it.

6 Choose OK. Excel searches the directories as you specified and presents a list of matching files.

7 Use the buttons at the bottom of the screen to manipulate the files in the list, such as opening them or previewing them. All Excel 5 files can be viewed in the **Preview** window before you open them.

Tip

You also can access the Find File dialog box through the Open dialog box by clicking the Find File button.

To start a new workbook using a template

1 Choose File New or press Ctrl+N to display the New dialog box.

2 Double-click the name of the template in the New list box.

Note

To make your template appear in the New dialog box, you must save the template into the C:\EXCEL\XLSTART directory using the Template file type in the Save As dialog box. See *Templates*.

To close a file

1 Choose File Close or double-click the Control menu located in the upper left corner of the workbook window (not the program window).

2 If you have made changes to the file or if the file is new, Excel prompts you to save the changes before closing. Choose Yes to save the changes.

3 If, in step 2, you are saving a new file, the Save As dialog box appears. Enter a name in the File Name text box and choose OK.

To minimize a workbook window

Click the Minimize button that appears in the upper right corner of the workbook window. If the workbook window is maximized, you will need to restore the window first. Do this by clicking the Restore button that appears in the upper right corner of the workbook window.

To save a workbook

1 Choose File Save.

Shortcut

 Press Ctrl+S. You also can click the Save button that appears on the Standard toolbar.

---

2 If the file is new, you will be asked to name the file. Use the Save As dialog box to select a directory from the **Directories** list box, then enter a name for the workbook in the File Name text box and choose OK.

To save a backup copy

1 Choose File Save As to display the Save As dialog box.

2 Type a new name for the file in the File Name text box. If you are saving to another drive, select a new drive in the Drives drop-down list box. Specify the desired directory for the backup copy if different from the current directory by clicking the directory in the Directories list box.

3 Choose OK.

4 If you want to work on the original file, return to it by selecting its name from the bottom of the File menu.

Tip

You can tell Excel to create a backup copy of the file each time you save it—without having to go through the preceding steps. To do this, choose **File Save As** and click the **O**ptions button to display the Save Options dialog box. Finally, click the Always Create **B**ackup check box and choose OK.

To save summary information

1 Choose **File** Summary **Info**.

2 Enter the summary information (**T**itle, **S**ubject, Author, **K**eywords, and **C**omments) into the Summary Info dialog box that appears.

3 Choose OK to save this information with the file.

Tip

You can instruct Excel to prompt you for summary information when you save a file. Choose **T**ools **O**ptions. Click the General tab, and then check the **P**rompt for Summary Info check box.

To save a file under a different name

1 Choose **File** Save **As**. The Save As dialog box appears.

2 Type a new name for the file in the File **N**ame text box. Specify the desired directory if different from the current directory by clicking on the directory in the **D**irectories list box.

3 Choose OK.

Note

If you want to work on the original file, return to it by selecting its name from the bottom of the File menu.

Filling a Range with Values

Excel offers AutoFill, a time-saving feature that enables you to create sequences of values instantly. This feature enables you to generate date sequences or numeric sequences without having to type each number or date. Just type the first two values and Excel figures out the sequence you have started and carries it forward or backward as far as you like.

To create a sequence of numbers

1 Type the first two numbers into the first two cells of the desired range. If you want a series of numbers starting with the number 1, enter 1 into the first cell and 2 into the second. If you want a series of odd numbers, enter 1 and 3.

2 Highlight the two cells you created in step 1.

3 Click and drag on the bottom right corner of the selection. As you click this corner called the fill handle, the mouse pointer changes to a "crosshair" shape. Drag down to create the sequence in a column. Drag to the right to create the sequence in a row. When you release the mouse button, the numerical sequence fills the cells you highlighted.

Tip

If you drag a sequence upward or to the left, you will create a sequence in reverse order. If your starting number is 1, for example, the sequence will go backward: 1, 0, -1, -2, and so on.

To create a sequence of dates

1 Type the first two dates into the first two cells of the desired range. If you want a series of dates to increase by months, starting with 1/1/93, type the dates **1/1/93** and **2/1/93** into the first two cells of the range. If you want to increase the sequence by years, type **1/1/93** and **1/1/94**. If you want to increase the sequence by days, you can actually just enter the first date into the first cell and skip the second entry.

2 Highlight the two cells you created in step 1.

3 Click and drag on the bottom right corner of the selection. As you click this corner called the fill handle, the mouse pointer changes to a "crosshair" shape. Drag down to create the sequence in a column. Drag to the right to create the sequence in a row. When you release the mouse, the date sequence fills the cells you highlighted.

To create a sequence of months

1 Type the first month into the first cell.

2 Drag the fill handle down or to the right to create a sequence.

To repeat (duplicate) numeric values

1 Type the numbers into the desired cells.

2 Highlight the cells used in step 1.

3 Hold down the Ctrl key, and then click and drag on the bottom right corner of the selection. As you click this corner called the fill handle, the mouse pointer changes to a "crosshair" shape with an additional crosshair in its upper right corner. Drag down to duplicate the values in a column. Drag to the right to duplicate the values in a row.

Finding Data

When your worksheets get large and are filled with data, you may have trouble finding specific information in them. Excel's Edit Find command enables you to jump to any piece of information in your workbook. You can even perform global search and replace procedures to change information throughout a worksheet.

To find data in your worksheet

1 Move the cell pointer to cell A1 to begin searching at the top of the worksheet. Otherwise, position the pointer where you would like to begin searching. You also can highlight a specific range to search only within that range.

2 Choose Edit Find or press Ctrl+F. The Find dialog box appears.

3 In the Find What text box, type the information you want to find.

4 In the Search drop-down list box, choose whether you want to search By Rows or By Columns.

5 Choose a category from the Look in drop-down list box. Formulas searches for your information in formula cells only. Values searches in non-formula cells and Notes searches in cell notes only.

6 Click the Match Case check box if you want to find the data you typed exactly as you typed it—including the upper-and lowercase letters. Otherwise, Excel will ignore the case of the letters.

7 Click the Find Entire Cells Only check box if the data you entered is an entire cell entry. Otherwise, Excel will find the data you entered—even if it appears as part of a larger cell entry.

8 Click Find Next to find the first matching entry. Click Find Next again to find the next matching entry. Click Close when finished.

To replace data throughout the worksheet

1 Move the cell pointer to cell A1 to begin searching and replacing at the top of the worksheet. Otherwise, position the pointer where you would like to begin searching. You also can highlight a specific range to search and replace only within that range.

2 Choose Edit Replace or press Ctrl+H. The Replace dialog box appears.

3 Type the information you want to find in the Find What text box.

4 In the Search drop-down list box, choose whether you want to search By Rows or By Columns.

5 Click the Match Case check box if you want to find the data you typed exactly as you typed it—including the upper-and lowercase letters. Otherwise, Excel will ignore the case of the letters.

6 Click the Find Entire Cells Only check box if the data you entered is an entire cell entry. Otherwise, Excel will find the data you entered, even if it appears as part of a larger cell entry.

7 Enter the replacement data into the Replace with text box.

8 Click Find Next to find the first matching entry. Click Replace if you want to replace that occurrence or click Find Next to find the next matching entry. You also can click the Replace All button to replace all occurrences without looking at each one individually. Click Close when finished.

Fonts

Excel enables you to control the fonts used in your worksheets. *Fonts* are the type styles that apply to the data you enter. You can control the font of each cell individually if desired, or change fonts in ranges of cells. You also can change the default fonts used throughout a worksheet.

To change the font used in a cell or range

1 Highlight the cell or range you want to change.

2 Choose the font you want from the Font drop-down list on the Formatting toolbar.

3 Choose the desired point size from the Font Size list on the Formatting toolbar. The following figure shows different fonts and font sizes.

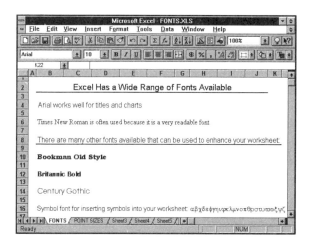

Tip

In addition to fonts and font sizes, you can change many character attributes of the data, such as making the type bold or italic. Most formatting options are available through the Format Cells command.

To change the default font of the current workbook

1 Choose Format Style. The Style dialog box appears.

2 Select the Normal style from the Style Name drop-down list box.

3 Click the Modify button. The Format Cells dialog box appears.

4 Click the Font tab if it's not already selected.

5 Change the font attributes you want.

6 Choose OK to return to the Style dialog box.

7 Choose OK again. (See also *Styles.*)

To change the default font in all new workbooks

1 Choose Tools Options. The Options dialog box appears.

2 Click the General tab.

3 Select the font you want from the Standard Font drop-down list box.

4 Select the font size you want from the Size drop-down list box.

5 Choose OK. Excel informs you that you must exit Excel and restart for these changes to take place.

6 Choose OK.

Formatting

To enhance the appearance and improve readability of your worksheets, you can format worksheet cells before or after you enter data. If you format before entering data, the data you enter will be in the new format. If you already have data in the cells, you must highlight a range, and then apply formatting.

The most common formatting tasks are represented by buttons on the Formatting toolbar, which is already active, by default.

Numbers

The default number format for a new worksheet is the General format, which displays up to 11 digits. Numbers display in the general format as: integers (123), decimal fractions (1.23), or if the number is longer than the cell width, scientific notation (1.23E+08). If you enter a different number style in a cell, such a dollar sign or percent sign, Excel's built-in number formatter changes the format from General to Currency or Percent.

Click one of the following five buttons on the Formatting toolbar to quickly change the format of a cell or selected range.

Button		Format
$	Currency	12345 becomes $12,345.00
%	Percent	.34 becomes 34%
,	Comma	56789 becomes 56,789.00
+.0 .00	Increase Decimal	12,345.00 becomes 12,345.000
.00 +.0	Decrease Decimal	12,345.00 becomes 12,345.0

To make other format changes to numbers:

1 Highlight a cell or range in which you want to change the number format.

2 Click the right mouse button on the cell or range to display the shortcut menu. Choose **F**ormat **C**ells to display the Format Cells dialog box.

3 Click the Number tab and click the Number format in the **C**ategory list box.

4 Click the various options in the **F**ormat Codes list box. Note the sample at the bottom of the dialog box that shows you how your number (or first cell of a range) looks in that format. Above the sample is the **Co**de text box. The highlighted format code also appears in this text box.

5 To create a custom format, find the format that most resembles what you want to create, clicking other items in the Category list box and Format Codes list box.

6 Click in the Code text box and edit the code, if desired. To find the meaning of the symbols used in the codes, click the Help button, and then choose Number Format Codes at the bottom of the Help window.

7 Choose OK.

See also *Alignment*, *Decimal Places*, and *Percentages*.

For an example of using conditional format codes to change the color of a number based on its value, see *Color*.

Text

To change the appearance of data (both text and values) in the worksheet, you can apply fonts, sizes, styles such as bold, italic, and underline, and color. You can make many of these changes using the buttons on the Formatting toolbar. A few more selections are available in the Format Cells dialog box. To change the default font of a workbook, or to set the default font in all new worksheets, see *Fonts*.

To change the font, size, and style for selected cells and numbers

1 Highlight the cell or range you want to change. Or, to change only particular characters in a cell, highlight the cell and then drag the mouse to highlight the characters of the text in the formula bar.

2  Click the arrow on the Font drop-down list box located on the Formatting toolbar. Use the scroll bar if necessary to find a font, and then select it.

3 Click the arrow on the Font Size drop-down list box, located on the Formatting toolbar. Click a point size. For some fonts, you can select in-between point sizes by typing the number in the Font Size box.

4 Select the style. On the Formatting toolbar, you can click the following buttons:

B Bold

I Italic

U Underline

These are toggle buttons, meaning that you can click them also to remove that style. You can choose any combination of these three styles. The following figure shows the different formatting styles you can use.

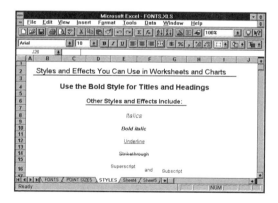

To change the color of font, see *Color.*

Other Font Characteristics

In addition to the font options available on the Formatting toolbar, you can choose strikethrough, superscript, subscript, and other underline styles in the Format Cells dialog box.

To change other font characteristics

1 Highlight the cell or range you want to change. Or to change only particular characters in a cell, highlight the cell and then drag the mouse to highlight the characters of the text in the formula bar.

2 Choose Format Cells or press Ctrl+1 to display the Format Cells dialog box.

3 Click the Font tab.

4 Choose the Font, Font Style, or Size list boxes to change any of these characteristics. These same options are available on the Formatting toolbar.

5 Choose the Underline drop-down list box to select an underline style, or None, to remove underlining.

6 Choose the Color drop-down list box to select a font color.

7 In the Effects area, you can choose Strikethrough, Superscript, or Subscript by clicking the appropriate check box.

8 To return all of the settings in this dialog box to Normal style which is set in the Style dialog box using the Format Style command, check the Normal Font check box.

9 A sample of all changes you make in this dialog box are shown in the Preview box. Choose OK to close the Format Cells dialog box.

See also *Alignment*, *Color*, and *Copying*.

Formulas

One of the most common tasks you will perform in Excel is creating formulas. Formulas enable you to calculate the values in the worksheet—add, subtract, multiply, and more.

To enter a formula

1 Move to the cell in which the formula is to appear.

2 Enter an equal sign (=).

3 Enter the expression that produces the result you want. An expression consists of operands, values, or variables (cell references) on which the expression operates and operators, symbols that represent mathematical procedures, such as a plus sign for addition. A formula can be simple, as in =A5+A6, or complex, as in =A5+((G5*2)/2)-A4. Formulas also can contain functions, as in =A5*SUM(C2:C5).

4 Press Enter when the formula is complete. As soon as you press Enter, Excel calculates the result of your formula and presents the result in the cell. The formula itself can be viewed in the Formula bar at the top of the screen when the cell pointer is on the appropriate cell. Errors in formulas produce error messages, which always begin with the pound sign, as in #NAME?. This error message indicates that you have used a range name that Excel does not recognize—or that you have incorrectly used text in your formulas and Excel thinks you're trying to specify a range name.

See also *Functions*, *Copying*, and *Naming Cells and Ranges*.

To enter a cell or range reference by pointing

1 Enter the desired formula up to the point of the cell or range reference. To enter the formula =A5+A6, for example, simply enter the equal sign =.

2 Use the arrow keys to move the cell pointer to the first cell reference. As you move the cell pointer, the formula tracks your progress and enters the current address into the formula.

3 When you reach the cell you want, press Enter to complete the formula or press the next element in the formula (such as the plus sign or another operator). Repeat these steps until the formula is complete.

> ### Tip
> You can point to a formula simply by clicking the mouse on the cell in step 2. Point to a range by dragging the mouse to highlight the desired range.

See also *Copying*, *Functions*, and *Selecting*.

Fractions

Excel enables you to work with fractional values in two different ways. You can use decimal values or fractions. Fractions appear with a slash (/) between the numerator and denominator and a space between the fractional value and the integer value, as in 3 1/3.

To enter a fractional value into a cell

1 Type the integer portion of the fraction first. If the value does not have an integer portion, type a zero.

2 Press the spacebar to enter a space after the integer, and then type the numerator and denominator of the fractional value, separated by a slash.

3 Press Enter.

To convert a fraction into a decimal

1 Highlight the cell containing the fraction.

2 Choose Format Cells, or press Ctrl+1. The Format Cells dialog box appears.

3 Click the Number tab.

4 Choose Number or Currency in the Category list box.

5 Choose a format in the Format Codes list box.

To convert a decimal into a fraction

1 Highlight the cell containing the decimal value.

2 Choose Format Cells or press Ctrl+1. The Format Cells dialog box appears.

3 Click the Number tab.

4 Select the Fraction category and choose one of the Fraction formats in the list provided. Choose OK when finished.

To align fractions in a column

1 Highlight the column of values containing fractions.

2 Choose Format Cells or press Ctrl+1. The Format Cells dialog box appears.

3 Click the Number tab.

4 Select Fraction from the Category list box.

5 In the Format Codes list box, choose the format # ??/??.

6 Choose OK.

Tip

If your fractions contain three-digit denominators, enter the custom number format # ???/??? to display these values.

Freeze Panes

When you are working in a large worksheet, you may want to lock other row or column headings so that you can see which row or column you are in. To do this, you must freeze the panes.

To freeze panes

1 To freeze horizontal (column) headings, highlight the row below your headings. To freeze vertical (row) headings, highlight the column to the right of the headings.

2 Choose **Window** Freeze Panes.

To unfreeze panes

Choose **Window** Unfreeze Panes.

Functions

Functions are special commands you type into your formulas that perform mathematical processes. By typing a single command, you can replace a series of formulas or expressions that would be required to produce the same result. For example, the AVERAGE function calculates the average of a range of cells—a result that would otherwise require you to calculate the total of all the cells, then divide the total by the number of cells. The NPV function calculates the net present value of a series of cash flows—an operation that most people would not even know how to perform with standard formulas.

Besides making complex operations simple, functions also can extend the powers of Excel. The IF function, for example, enables you to create logical expressions and perform one of two operations depending on a condition. An IF function could be used to create the expression: "If the value in cell A1 is greater than 100, then add to its value the values in cells C5 and C6 and enter the sum in the active cell, otherwise enter 'value too small' in the active cell." This function would appear as:

```
=IF(A1>100,(A1+C5+C6),"value too small")
```

Excel includes built-in worksheet functions so numerous that they are categorized to assist you in searching for the ones you need. The categories of functions include: Financial, Date & Time, Math & Trig, Statistical, Lookup & Reference, Database, Text, Logical, and Information. You also can define functions for calculations you use often in the User Defined category. In addition to displaying these categories and their component functions, the Excel Function Wizard also steps you through the particular *arguments* required for each function, then takes care of the syntax for you. The steps for using Function Wizard are included later in this section.

Entering Functions

To enter a function, you must type it, using the correct syntax, and then press Enter. The result of the formula appears in the worksheet cell.

Functions can be used only in formulas, so you must begin a function entry with an equal sign to start the formula—even if the function is the only expression in the formula. Functions always include parentheses after them; some functions require you to enter values (or arguments) into these parentheses, others just require empty parentheses. The function SUM, for example, requires a range of cells that you want to sum inside the parentheses, as in =SUM(A1:A10). However, the PI function requires no arguments, as in =PI( ).

See also *Formulas*.

Choosing the **I**nsert **F**unction command displays the Function Wizard - Step 1 of 2 dialog box. This is the equivalent of clicking the Function Wizard button on the Standard toolbar.

To enter functions directly into the worksheet cell

1 Highlight the cell in which the formula will be entered.

2 Type an equal sign to start the formula. Note that the formula bar buttons appear, anticipating the entry of the formula.

3 Enter the function name, followed by a left parenthesis, arguments as required for this function, and a right parenthesis. You can type the function and cell references in upper- or lowercase. Excel will convert letters to uppercase.

4 Press Enter. If the formula was entered without any errors, the cell will have the result of the function entered. If you make the cell active again, you will see the function in the formula bar.

Note

If you are having trouble finding an error in the function you have entered, use Function Wizard to debug it. With the problem cell highlighted, click the Function Wizard button on the formula bar or Standard toolbar. See one of the following sections, "Using the Function Wizard to enter a function."

You also can enter or edit a function in the formula bar by selecting the cell that will contain the function, and then clicking in the entry area of the formula bar. Start with an equal sign and type the function, just as described in steps above.

With either of these entry methods, you can click the enter box in the formula bar (the one with a green check mark) or press enter to complete the entry. Click the cancel box (the one with the red X) to cancel your entry and start over.

Tip

You can paste argument names directly into a function formula without activating Function Wizard. Type the equal sign and function name then press Ctrl+Shift+A. If you entered =**PMT**, the result in the cell is =PMT(rate,nper,pv,fv,type). Edit the argument names then press Enter.

To add a row or column using AutoSum

1 Highlight a cell adjacent to a row or column of numbers you want to add.

2 Click the AutoSum button on the Standard toolbar. Excel supplies the =SUM( ) formula with a suggested range for the sum: the column above or row to the left of the selected cell.

3 If the range is correct, click the AutoSum button again or press Enter to complete the entry. If the range supplied by AutoSum is incorrect, highlight the desired range before pressing Enter.

You also can double-click the AutoSum button to total the column above or row to the left of the active cell.

Enter multiple SUM( ) functions simultaneously by highlighting the range where the totals will be, or by highlighting the entire range of cells to be summed, then clicking the AutoSum button once.

Enter totals at the bottom and right side of a range at the same time. Highlight the numeric range and the surrounding blank cells where you want the totals to be entered. Click the AutoSum button once.

To use the Function Wizard to enter a function

1 Highlight the cell into which the formula is to appear.

2 Type an equal sign to start the formula.

3 Enter any expression that appears before the function.

4 When you are ready to enter the function, click the Function Wizard button on the Standard toolbar. The Function Wizard - Step 1 of 2 dialog box appears.

5 Choose a function category from the Function **Cat**egory list box on the left side of the dialog box. Functions within that category appear on the right.

6 Locate the function you want in the Function **Name** list box. Note that the bottom of the dialog box displays a brief description of the selected function. Use the down arrow to select other functions. After you find and select the function you want, click the Next button. The Function Wizard - Step 2 of 2 dialog box appears.

7 Fill in any values required for the function. These are the function's arguments. Use the Tab key to move among the various arguments that are required. Some functions require several arguments, others require none. The dialog box informs you what each argument represents and what type of information is required for the argument. One argument might require that you enter a range of cells while another argument requires a single value. Whenever you are asked to enter a value for an argument, you can enter the value right inside the text box or click the worksheet to "point" to a cell or range containing the value. Whenever you see the Function Wizard button beside an argument text box, this indicates that you can click the button to select another function as the argument to the current function—creating a nested set of functions.

8 When all the arguments are satisfied, click the **F**inish button to enter the function and its arguments into the current cell.

9 Make any changes desired in the formula bar or extend the formula with additional expressions, and then press Enter to complete the entry.

Grid Lines

Grid lines appear on the Excel screen and are printed, by default. If you prefer not to see the grid lines, you can turn them off. Turning them off also tells Excel not to print the gridlines. If you want to see the gridlines, but not print them, you can do that as well.

To turn off gridlines

1 Choose Tools Options. The Options dialog box appears.

2 Click the View tab.

3 In the Window Options area, uncheck the **G**ridlines check box.

4 Choose OK. The grid lines do not appear on-screen or print.

┌─ **Tip** ─────────────────────────────
│ To choose a color for the gridlines, click the
│ Color drop-down list box and then choose a
│ color.
└──────────────────────────────────────

To turn off gridlines so they don't print

1 Choose File Page Set**u**p. The Page Setup dialog box appears.

2 Click the Sheet tab.

3 In the Print area, uncheck the **G**ridlines check box.

4 Choose OK.

┌─ **Note** ─────────────────────────────
│ To turn gridlines back on, follow the same
│ steps. This time be sure that an X appears
│ in the Gridlines check box.
└──────────────────────────────────────

Headers and Footers

When you print your worksheet, you can include a header or footer on the printout. A header appears at the top of the page; a footer appears at the bottom. You might want to include the file name, the report name, page numbers, or dates in a header or footer.

By default, Excel prints the worksheet name in the header and the page number in the footer. If you don't want anything to print, delete the entries. By default, headers are printed 1/2-inch from the top of the page, and footers 1/2-inch from the bottom.

To use a predefined header or footer

1 Choose File Page Setup. The File Setup dialog box appears.

2 Click the Header/Footer tab.

3 Click the arrow next to the Header drop-down list box, and then choose one of the predefined formats. To use a predefined footer, click the arrow next to the Footer drop-down list box, and then select a predefined footer.

4 Choose OK.

> ## Tip
> A sample of the header and footer appear in the dialog box. Check this to be sure you like what you see.

To create a custom header or footer

1 Choose File Page Setup. The File Setup dialog box appears.

2 Click the Header/Footer tab.

3 Choose the Custom Header button to create a customized header, or choose Custom Footer to create a customized footer.

4 Click in the text box in which you want to enter text. You can enter text in the **Left**, **Center**, and **Right** sections of the header or footer.

5 Enter the text and codes you want. To insert a code, click the buttons that appear in the dialog box. Following is what each button does:

Button	Description
[A] Font	Changes the font of highlighted text or text to be entered.
[#] Page Number	Inserts page number.
[+] Total Pages	Inserts number of pages (for example, you can print Page 1 of 12 using this button and the preceding button).
[ ] Date	Inserts the date.
[ ] Time	Inserts the time.
[ ] Filename	Inserts the file name.
[ ] Sheet Name	Inserts the worksheet name.

6 Choose OK.

To delete a header or footer

1 Choose **File Page Setup**. The Page Setup dialog box appears.

2 Click the Header/Footer tab.

3 Click the arrow next to the Header or Footer drop-down list box.

4 Choose (none).

5 Choose OK.

To change the header and footer margins

1 Choose File Page Setup. The Page Setup dialog box appears.

2 Click the Margins tab.

3 Click in the Header or Footer spin box in the From Edge area.

4 Click the spin box arrows to change the margin settings.

5 Choose OK.

Help

Excel offers an extensive on-line help program. You can display a help index and select a topic, search for help on a particular topic, get context-sensitive help, and more. If you cannot remember how to perform some task, use Excel's help system to tell you how.

To display help on a topic

1 Choose Help Contents or press F1. The Microsoft Excel Help window appears.

2 Click the category you want. If the entry is under-lined or appears in a different color, that means the category or topic is available. You can jump to these topics. If the entry is underlined with a dashed line, you can display a definition of the term by clicking the word or phrase.

3 Click the topic you want.

4 Continue selecting topics until the help information appears. To scroll through the help window, click the scroll arrows.

5 After you finish reading the help information, double-click the Control menu box to close the Help window.

> **Tip**
>
> To move backwards through the selections, click the **B**ack button at the top of the Help window.

To search for help

1 Choose **Help S**earch for Help on. The Search dialog box appears.

> **Shortcut**
>
> You also can click the **S**earch button in the Help Contents window.

2 Type the name of the feature for which you want help or click the topic you want in the topics list.

3 Click the **S**how Topics button.

4 Choose the topic you want in the Select a **t**opic list box.

5 Click the **G**o To button.

6 After you finish reading the help information, double-click the Control menu box to close the Help window.

To get context-sensitive help

1 Click the Help button on the Standard toolbar. The cursor changes to a question mark.

2 Click the command or menu item for which you want to get help. The Microsoft Excel Help window appears, displaying help on the selected command.

3 After you finish reading the help information, double-click the Control menu box to close the Help window.

Tip

Most dialog boxes include a **Help** button. If
you are unsure what to do, click this button
to display help for the particular dialog box.

Hiding Data

A worksheet may contain certain elements—a column,
an object, a range—that you don't want to appear on the
worksheet. If so, you can hide that element. Hidden
elements don't print when you print the worksheet.

Columns, Rows, and Worksheets

You easily can hide columns, rows, or worksheets with
Excel commands or with the mouse.

To hide columns

1 Select the column you want to hide by clicking the
   column heading. After selecting one column, you
   can select other columns by pressing the Ctrl key
   while clicking each column heading.

2 Choose Format Column.

3 From the Format Column menu, choose **Hide**.

Shortcut

You also can press Ctrl+0 (zero) to accomplish steps 2 and 3.

Tip

To use the mouse to hide a column, place
the mouse pointer on the right column border. Drag the right column border past the
left column border.

To redisplay hidden columns

1 Highlight the two columns on either side of the hidden column. If column C is hidden, for example, highlight columns B and D.

2 Choose Format Column.

3 From the Format Column menu, choose Unhide.

> ## Tip
>
> To use the mouse to unhide a column, place the mouse pointer between two column headings next to the hidden column. If column C is hidden, for example, place the mouse pointer between column headings B and D. Move the mouse pointer around until it turns from a single thick border to a double-lined border. Then drag the column border to the right.

To hide rows

1 Highlight the row you want to hide by clicking the row heading. After selecting one row, you can highlight other rows by pressing the Ctrl key while clicking each row heading.

2 Choose Format Row.

3 From the Format Row menu, choose Hide.

> ## Shortcut
>
> You also can press Ctrl+9 to accomplish steps 2 and 3.

To redisplay hidden rows

1 Highlight the two rows on either side of the hidden row. If row 3 is hidden, for example, highlight rows 2 and 4.

2 Choose Format Row.

3 From the Format Row menu, choose Unhide.

┌─ **Shortcut** ─────────────────────────────
│
│ You also can press Ctrl+Shift+(to accom-
│ plish steps 2 and 3.
│
└──

To hide worksheets

1 Select the sheet you want to hide by clicking the
sheet tab.

2 Choose Format Sheet.

3 From the Format Sheet menu, choose Hide.

To redisplay hidden worksheets

1 Choose Format Sheet.

2 From the Format Sheet menu, choose Unhide. Excel
displays the Unhide dialog box listing the hidden
sheets.

3 In the Unhide Sheet list box, click the sheet you
want to unhide.

4 Choose OK.

Screen Elements

You can customize the Excel screen to display just the
elements you want. If you don't want the toolbar or
scroll bars to appear on-screen, for example, you can
hide them.

To hide the formula bar

Choose View Formula Bar. When a check mark appears next to this command, the bar appears on-
screen. Removing the check mark hides the formula
bar.

To hide the status bar

Choose View Status Bar. When a check mark appears next to this command, the bar appears on-
screen. Removing the check mark hides the status
bar.

To hide toolbars

1 Choose View **T**oolbars to display the Toolbars dialog box. When an X appears in the check box next to
the toolbar name, that toolbar appears on-screen.

2 Uncheck all toolbars you want to hide by clicking
the corresponding check box.

3 Choose OK.

To hide other on-screen elements

1 Choose Tools **O**ptions. The Options dialog box
appears.

2 Click the View tab.

3 In the Show area, choose the element you want to
display. (An X in the check box means the item will
appear on-screen.) Here are the options:

Formula Bar	Uncheck this check box to hide the formula bar.
Status Bar	Uncheck this check box to hide the status bar.
Note Indicator	Uncheck this check box to hide the note indicator. The note indicator is a small red box that appears in cells with notes attached.
Info **W**indow	Displays a window with information about the selected cell.

4 In the Object area, choose the way in which you
want objects to appear.

Show **A**ll	Shows all objects.
Show **P**laceholders	Shows gray box where object appears.
Hi**d**e All	Hides all objects.

5 In the Window Options area, choose which items you want to appear:

Automatic Page Breaks	Check this check box if you want to see page breaks on-screen.
Formulas	Check this check box to see formulas rather than results.
Gridlines	Uncheck this check box to hide the gridlines.
Row & Column Headers	Uncheck this check box to hide the row and column headings.
Outline Symbols	Uncheck this check box to hide outline symbols. (Outline symbols only appear when you have created an outline.)
Zero Values	Uncheck this check box to hide cells that contain 0.
Horizontal Scroll Bars	Uncheck this check box to hide the horizontal scroll bars.
Vertical Scroll Bars	Uncheck this check box to hide the vertical scroll bars.
Sheet Tabs	Uncheck this check box to hide the sheet tabs.

6 Choose OK.

Objects

You can include objects (a chart, a picture) in your worksheet. If you don't want these objects displayed or printed, you can hide them.

Tip

When you make a change to the worksheet, Excel sometimes needs to redraw the screen. Redrawing pictures and objects can zap system resources. To save time, hide the objects when you are editing the worksheet. Then when you are ready to print, redisplay the objects.

To hide objects

1 Choose Tools Options. The Options dialog box appears.

2 Click the View tab.

3 In the Objects area, choose the Hide All option button.

Tip

To display a placeholder (a gray box) for the object, choose the Show Placeholders option button.

4 Choose OK.

Shortcut

To alternatively show placeholders, hide all objects, and show all objects, press Ctrl+6 repeatedly.

To unhide objects

1 Choose Tools Options. The Options dialog box appears.

2 Click the View tab.

3 In the Objects area, select the Show All or Show Placeholders option button.

4 Choose OK.

Chart Elements

The Chart toolbar includes buttons that enable you to hide the horizontal lines in the plot area and the legend in a chart.

To hide the gridlines or legend

1 Click the chart to select it.

2 To hide the horizontal lines, click the Horizontal Gridlines button on the Chart toolbar.

3 To hide the legend, click the Legend button on the Chart toolbar.

> **Note**
>
> To redisplay the items, click the button again.

In-Cell Editing

New in Excel Version 5 is the capability to edit your data right inside the cell. You can add, remove, or change information you previously typed into a cell by double-clicking the cell and changing the information. You also can use the old method of editing data, which involves the formula bar at the top of the screen. To access the formula bar, press F2 or click the formula bar.

To add to an existing entry

1 Double-click the desired cell.

2 Click inside the cell's data to position the cursor (if you want to add data to the end of the cell, skip this step and go to step 3).

3 Begin typing.

4 Press Enter when you are finished.

To delete or change parts of an entry

1 Double-click the desired cell.

2 Click and drag within the cell contents to highlight the data you want to remove or change.

3 To remove the data, press Delete. To change the data, type the new information and it will replace the highlighted data.

4 Press Enter when finished.

To break lines within the formula bar of a cell

1 Double-click the cell.

2 Click where you would like to start a new line. This positions the cursor at the beginning of that line.

3 Press Alt+Enter. Repeat steps 2 and 3 to break other lines.

4 Press Enter.

Note

When you break the lines of a text entry, Excel automatically wraps all text inside the cell using the **W**rap Text option on the Alignment tab of the Format Cells dialog box. When you break the lines of a formula, Excel does not wrap the text. Breaking lines of a formula is a good way to display the flow of complex formulas. You can indent lines of a formula by pressing Ctrl+Alt+Tab at the beginning of the line.

Inserting

As you edit your worksheet, you may need to insert data in places. Perhaps you forgot a category you want to include in a column, or maybe you need to insert a row.

Excel makes it easy to insert data, columns, rows, and worksheets. You can insert rows, columns, or ranges into your worksheets at any time. This may be necessary if you need more space within a worksheet report area or analysis area. You also can insert new worksheets into the workbook.

To insert rows or columns

1 Highlight the row you want to move down when you insert the new row(s). Or, highlight the column you want to move to the right when the new column(s) is inserted.

2 Highlight additional rows or columns to indicate the number of rows or columns you want to insert. If you want to insert four rows, for example, highlight the next three rows below the one you selected in step 1. Highlight additional rows or columns by holding the Shift key down and clicking the last column in the group.

3 Choose **Insert Columns** or **Insert Rows** to insert the desired element. Existing data will move right or down to accommodate the new cells.

To insert cells or ranges

1 Highlight the cell where you want to insert a new cell.

2 Choose **Insert Cells**. The Insert dialog box appears.

3 Choose one of the following:

Shift Cells **R**ight	Shifts existing cells to the right and inserts one cell.
Shift Cells **D**own	Shifts existing cells down and inserts one cell.
Entire **R**ow	Shifts all cells in that row down and inserts a new row.
Entire **C**olumn	Shifts all cells in that column to the right and inserts a new column.

4 Choose OK.

To insert worksheets

1 Select the worksheet where you want to insert the new worksheet by clicking the sheet tab. The new worksheet will be inserted before this worksheet.

2 Choose Insert Worksheet or press Shift+F11.

Installing Excel

Installing Microsoft Excel 5.0 for Windows is easy. Just start the Setup program and follow the on-screen instructions. You must install this software on a hard disk.

To install Excel for Windows

1 Start Microsoft Windows; place the disk labeled "Disk 1 - Setup" in drive A. (If you install from a different drive, substitute that drive's letter.)

2 Choose File Run from the Program Manager menu. The Run dialog box appears.

3 Type **a:setup** in the Command Line text box.

4 Choose OK.

5 Follow the Setup instructions on the screen.

Italic

See *Formatting*

Lines

See *Borders*

Linking Dynamically

Linking is the process of dynamically updating data in a worksheet from data in another source worksheet. Because the data is linked, any changes you make to the original data are reflected in the linked versions. Linking is accomplished through special formulas that contain references known as *external references*. An external reference can refer to a cell in a different worksheet in the same workbook, or any other worksheet in any other workbook.

To link data from other worksheets

1 Highlight a cell in the first worksheet to which data from the second worksheet is to be linked.

2 Type an equal sign (=) to begin a formula entry.

3 Click the sheet tab to switch to the second worksheet (the worksheet that contains the data you want to link to the first worksheet.)

4 Click the cell in the second worksheet containing the data you want to link.

5 Press Enter. The result is a linking formula in the first worksheet that follows the syntax =Sheet!Cell, where Sheet is the name of the external worksheet and Cell is any cell in that worksheet. The formula =January!C5, for example, links cell C5 in the January sheet to the worksheet containing the formula.

To link data from other workbooks

1 Open the two workbooks that are to be linked.

2 Use the **Window** menu to select the first workbook that is to contain the linking formula. This formula will refer to a cell in the second workbook.

3 Click the sheet tab to select the worksheet, if it is not already active, then highlight the cell that will contain the formula.

4 Type an equal sign (=) to begin the formula.

5 Use the **W**indow menu to switch to the second workbook.

6 Select the worksheet, if it is not already active, and then click the cell that contains the data you want to link to the first workbook.

7 Press Enter. The result is a linking formula that contains an external reference to the second workbook. The syntax is: [Book]Sheet!Cell, where *Book* is the name of the external workbook, *Sheet* is the name of the worksheet within that workbook, and *Cell* is a cell within the worksheet.

Updating Links

If both worksheets are open, links, by default, are updated automatically. If the data in the source workbook is changed while the dependent workbook—the one which contains a link formula—was closed, then the linked data has not yet been updated. Excel will inquire next time you open the dependent workbook whether you want to update now. Choose **Y**es to update all of the linked data in the workbook. If you choose **N**o, or if you have links that are manually updated, you can update the links.

To update links

1 Choose **E**dit Lin**k**s to display the Links dialog box.

2 The Source file list box contains a list of all linking references used in the active worksheet. Click the link reference you want to update or edit.

3 Choose the **U**pdate Now button to update the link; this button is unavailable if data is already current. In the Link dialog box, you also can click the **C**hange Source button to change the link reference or open the source worksheet by clicking the **O**pen button.

4 Choose OK.

Macros and Custom Controls

Macros are special instructions that control Excel.
By typing a series of macro instructions into a macro
module, or macro sheet in the workbook, you can make
Excel perform any series of commands or actions for
you. Anything you could accomplish in Excel through
use of the mouse or keyboard can be automated in a
macro. That is, the macro will cause Excel to accomplish
the task by itself. You simply "show" Excel what you
want to accomplish while the macro is "recording" your
actions. Then, Excel can repeat the task at any time by
itself. Macros are useful for automating repetitive or
complex tasks you intend to perform repeatedly.
Although a macro is a series of programming instructions, you need not know anything about programming
to create them. Excel offers a macro recording feature
that translates your actions into macro instructions.
The following sections show you how to automate Excel
through macros and custom controls.

Creating a Macro

You can create a macro by recording your actions.
The macro recorder translates your actions into macro
instructions and places them onto a new macro module.
If you can perform an action in Excel, you can create a
macro that will perform the action for you.

To record a macro

1 Choose **T**ools **R**ecord Macro.

2 From the Tools Record Macro menu, choose **R**ecord
New Macro. The Record New Macro dialog box
appears.

3 Type a name for the macro in the **M**acro Name text
box.

4 In the **D**escription text box, you see the default description. The default description uses the date and
user name. Press Tab and enter a different description for the macro, if desired.

5 Choose OK to begin recording.

6 Perform the actions you want the macro to record. Every move you make is recorded by Excel until you stop the macro.

7 When you are finished with the recording, click the Stop button on the Stop Recording toolbar that appears on the screen, or choose the **T**ools **R**ecord Macro **S**top Recording command.

To assign a macro to a shortcut key

1 Choose **T**ools **M**acro to display the Macro dialog box.

2 Click the name of the macro to which you want to assign a shortcut key.

3 Click the **O**ptions button to display the Macro Options dialog box.

4 In the Assign To area, click to place an X in the Shortcut **K**ey check box, and then type a letter into the **C**trl+ text box. This is the key combination that will invoke the macro.

5 Choose OK to return to the Macro dialog box.

6 Choose Close.

┌─ **Tip** ─────────────────────────────
│ To invoke the macro with the shortcut key,
│ press the Ctrl key and the letter you en-
│ tered, such as Ctrl+A.
└──────────────────────────────────────

To assign a macro to a custom command on the Tools menu

1 Choose **T**ools **M**acro to display the Macro dialog box.

2 Click the name of the macro to which you want to assign a command on the **T**ools menu.

3 Click the **O**ptions button.

4   In the Assign To area, click to place an X in the Menu
    Item on Tools Menu check box, and then enter a
    name in the adjacent text box that will appear in the
    menu for running the macro. You can use the name
    of the macro itself or any other name that reminds
    you of the macro's purpose.

5   Click OK.

6   Click Close.

To edit a macro

1   Choose Tools Macro to display the Macro dialog
    box.

2   In the Macro Name/Reference list box, click the
    name of the macro you want to edit.

3   Click the Edit button. The Visual Basic module sheet
    appears, containing the code for the selected macro.
    Note that the Visual Basic toolbar also appears.

4   Edit the macro as desired by clicking the insertion
    point on the text you want to edit.

5   When finished editing the macro, you can click any
    sheet tab to exit the macro module.

Running a Macro

Once you have recorded a macro, you can run it at any
time. Excel provides many ways to run macros. In
addition, you can run a macro by attaching it to a
custom control as explained later in this section.

To run a macro using the Tools Macro command

1   Choose Tools Macro to display the Macro dialog
    box.

2   In the Macro Name/Reference list box, click the
    name of the macro you want to run.

3   Click the Run button.

To run a macro assigned to a shortcut key

    Press Ctrl+ the letter you assigned.

To run a macro from a custom menu

Choose the macro from the **T**ools menu.

Creating Custom Controls

Custom controls are Windows screen elements that help you control your worksheet values and operations. Primarily, you use them to help make your worksheets easier to use by others and yourself. Suppose that your bookkeeping worksheet tracks all expenses for your company. When you enter an expense transaction, you must also enter the accounting code to which it applies. Rather than remembering the codes, you can place a list box on-screen and choose a code from the list box. Controls include check boxes, option buttons, list boxes, scroll bars, and spinners (also referred to as *spin boxes*). Check boxes enable you to present a series of and/or options. Option buttons enable you to create either/or options. List boxes enable you to present a series of items from which you can choose. Scroll bars and spinners enable you to present a range of values from which to choose. To create custom controls, you must first display the Forms toolbar, which you can access using the **V**iew **T**oolbars command. Check the Forms check box in the **T**oolbars list box in the **T**oolbars dialog box, and then choose OK.

To create check boxes

1 ☒ From the Forms toolbar, click the Check Box button.

2 Click and drag on the worksheet to create the check box. The check box appears in a text box.

3 Click and drag on the text box text to highlight it, and then type the name of the first check box to replace the default text.

4 You can draw more check boxes to complete the number of options you want to make available.

5 You can move a custom control object by right-clicking the control to select it, and then left-clicking the border of the control and dragging the object.

Use this process to arrange the text boxes properly. Do not change the order of the check boxes.

6 Right-click the first check box and choose Format Object from the shortcut menu. The Format Object dialog box appears.

7 Click the Control tab and click the Cell Link text box.

8 Enter a cell address into the Cell Link text box or click the worksheet to "point" to the desired cell. The cell you identify will contain the value TRUE if the check box is checked and FALSE if the check box is not checked. You then can use worksheet functions, such as the IF function, to respond to these values and perform operations on the worksheet.

9 Choose OK.

10 Repeat steps 6 through 9 for the remaining check boxes.

To create option buttons

1 From the Forms toolbar, click the Option Button button.

2 Click and drag on the worksheet to create the option button. The option button appears in a text box.

3 Click and drag the text box text to highlight it. Now type the name of the first option to replace the default text.

Tip

If you want to edit the text later, you can right-click the text box to select it, and then left-click and drag over the text inside the box. If, when you right-click the object the shortcut menu covers up the object, right-click more toward the right side of the object.

---

4 Draw more option buttons to complete the options available. (You can draw as many as you need.)

5 You can move a custom control object by right-clicking the control to select it, and then left-clicking on the border of the control and dragging the object. Use this process to arrange the text boxes properly. Do not change the order of the option buttons. Excel remembers the order in which you drew the option buttons and numbers the option buttons accordingly.

6 Right-click the first option button and choose Format Object from the shortcut menu. The Format Object dialog box appears.

7 Click the Control tab and click the Cell Link text box.

8 Enter a cell address into the Cell Link text box or click the worksheet to "point" to the desired cell. The cell you identify will contain the number of the option button selected. You then can use worksheet functions, such as the IF function, to respond to this value and perform operations on the worksheet.

9 Choose OK.

To create list boxes

1 From the Forms toolbar, click one of the four list box buttons: List Box button and choose List Box, Drop-Down, Combination List-Edit, Drop-Down Edit.

2 Click and drag onto the worksheet to create the list box control.

3 You can move a custom control object by right-clicking the control to select it, and then left-clicking on the border of the control and dragging the object.

4 Right-click the list box and choose the Format Object command from the shortcut menu. The Format Object dialog box appears.

5 Click the Control tab.

6 Click the Input Range text box and type a reference to the range containing the desired items for the list box. If you do not have a range on the worksheet that contains the items for the list, highlight a blank range, and then enter the items into that range later. You can use a range name if the range is already named.

7 In the Cell Link text box, type a cell reference or point to a cell not in the above input range, in which the value of the selected list item is to be returned. Excel returns the value 1 if the first item in the list box is chosen, 2 if the second item is chosen, and so on. You then can use worksheet functions, such as the IF function, to respond to this value and perform operations on the worksheet.

8 For drop-down list boxes, enter the number of lines you want the list to display in the Drop Down Lines text box. If the list contains more items than you have indicated in the Drop Down Lines text box, the list will scroll to allow more items to be seen.

9 Click OK.

To create a scroll bar or spinner

1 From the Forms toolbar, click the Scroll Bar button or the Spinner button.

2 Click and drag on the worksheet to create the button. Note that scroll bar controls should be drawn as a long rectangle and the spinner control can be more square.

> **Tip**
>
> You can move a custom control object by right-clicking the control to select it, and then left-clicking on the border of the control and dragging the object.

3 Right-click the control and choose Format Object from the shortcut menu. The Format Object dialog box appears.

4 Click the Control tab.

5 Enter the minimum and maximum values for the tool into the **M**inimum Value and Ma**x**imum Value spin boxes. This indicates the low and high range of the button.

6 Enter the incremental change into the **I**ncremental Change spin box. This indicates how fast the control will move (by how many increments) when you click the controls. Enter the **P**age Change value for scroll bars, to indicate the amount of jump that occurs when you click the scroll box rather than the scroll arrows.

7 Enter a cell reference in the Cell **L**ink text box or click a worksheet cell. Excel returns the value of the scroll bar or spinner control to this cell. This is useful for entering values into the worksheet.

8 To turn off 3-D shading, uncheck the **3**D Shading check box

9 Choose OK.

Attaching Macros to Controls

You can attach macros to your custom controls. This enables you to invoke a macro by using the control. To attach a macro to a control, be sure that you have a working macro ready to use.

To insert custom menu commands into Excel's menus

1 Display the Visual Basic toolbar choosing **V**iew **T**oolbars. Check the Visual Basic check box in the Toolbars list box in the Toolbars dialog box, and then choose OK.

2 Click the Menu Editor button on the Visual Basic toolbar to display the Menu Editor dialog box.

3 Use the Menu **B**ars drop-down list box to select the menu bar you want to change. The Worksheet menu bar is the normal bar that appears when you are working on a worksheet.

4 Click a menu in the **M**enus list box. This is the menu you want to change, or you can insert a new menu prior to this one on the menu bar. To insert a new menu, click the **I**nsert button and enter a menu name into the **C**aption text box and press Tab. The new menu name appears in the menu list. You now can click the new menu to select it and add commands to it.

5 To insert a new menu item, click the desired item in the Menu **I**tems list (or click the End of Menu item to insert an item at the end of the menu) and click the **I**nsert button. Next, enter the item name into the **C**aption text box and press Tab. This enters the new menu command above the one you selected.

6 Click the new command you inserted into the menu to select it.

7 Choose a macro from the **M**acro drop-down list box. This is the macro that will run when the menu command is selected.

8 Choose OK. The new menu should appear in the menu bar.

To attach a macro to a graphic object or worksheet button

1 Right-click the button to select it.

2 Click Assign Macro from the shortcut menu. The Assign Macro dialog box appears.

3 Choose the macro from the **M**acro Name/Reference list box.

4 Choose OK.

To attach a macro to a custom Toolbar button

1 Display the toolbar into which you want the new button inserted by choosing **V**iew **T**oolbars to display the Toolbars dialog box. In the Toolbars dialog box, click to place an X in the check box next to the toolbar name in the Toolbars list box. Choose OK.

2 Choose View Toolbars again and click the Customize button.

3 At the bottom of the Categories list box, click the Custom category.

4 Drag one of the custom buttons in the Button area into the desired toolbar and release the mouse. The tool will appear inside the toolbar and the Assign Macro dialog will appear.

5 In the Macro Name/Reference list box, click the macro you want to assign to the button.

6 Choose OK to return to the Customize dialog box.

7 Choose Close.

Margins

By default, Excel creates a 1-inch top and bottom margin and a .75-inch left and right margin. Headers and footers have a .5-inch margin. You can change these settings. You can change them in a dialog box, or if you prefer to change them visually, you can do so in Print Preview.

To change the margins

1 Choose File Page Setup. The Page Setup dialog box appears.

2 Click the Margins tab.

3 Click the margin spin box you want to change: Top, Bottom, Left, or Right.

4 Click the spin box arrows to change the margin settings.

5 Choose OK.

Tip

If you can't get your printout to look right
on the page, try centering it. Choose File
Page Setup, and then click the Margins tab.
You can choose to center the page horizontally or vertically by clicking the appropriate check box in the Center on Page area.

To change the header and footer margins

1 Choose File Page Setup. The Page Setup dialog box
appears.

2 Click the Margins tab.

3 Click the Header or Footer spin box in the From
Edge area.

4 Click the spin box arrows to change the margin
settings.

5 Choose OK.

To change the margins in Print Preview

1 Choose File Print Preview. The Print Preview window appears.

2 Select the Margins button. Dotted guidelines appear
to indicate each margin.

3 Click the margin guideline you want to change.

4 Drag the guideline to the new location.

Menus

Excel's menu system makes it easy to access the commands and features you want. The menu bar appears
along the top of the window. If you want to add your
own menu items, you can do that also.

> ## Tip
> Use the buttons on the toolbars if you want quick access to commands. See *Toolbars*.

Selecting Commands

You can use both the mouse and the keyboard to select commands. With some commands, a dialog box appears with additional options. You can select the options you want and choose OK to execute the command.

To select a command with the mouse

1 Click the menu name. A list of menu commands drops down.

2 Click the command you want.

3 If a dialog box appears, make the selections you want. Different dialog boxes contain different elements. Following are the most common elements, as well as how to make a selection:

Tab	Click the tab.
List box	Click the item you want in the list box.
Option buttons	Click the option button. When an option is selected, the button is darkened in the center. When the option is not selected, the button is blank. You can select only one option in each group of options.
Check boxes	Click the check box. When a check box is activated, an X appears. When a check box is not selected, it is blank. You can select more than one check box in a group of check boxes.

Text box	Click in the text box; then delete and retype the entry or edit the entry.
Spin box	Press Alt+ *the key letter* to select the spin box. Type your entry or click the up arrow to increase the value or click the down arrow to decrease the value.
Drop-down list box	Click the arrow next to the option name to display the drop-down list. Then click the list item you want.
Command buttons	Click the button you want. Clicking OK confirms the selections. Clicking Cancel closes the dialog box without making the changes.

To display shortcut menus

1 Select the items you want to modify. Depending on what you select, the shortcut menu will vary. Therefore, select what you want to work with first.

2 Press the right mouse button. A shortcut menu of options that pertain to the selection appears.

To select a command with the keyboard

1 Press Alt+*the underlined key letter* of the menu. The key letter is underlined on-screen.

2 Press the key letter of the command, or press the down arrow key to move to the command you want, and then press Enter.

> ## Tip
> Excel offers several keyboard shortcuts. If you prefer to keep your hands on the keyboard, take some time to learn some of the shortcuts. Shortcuts are displayed next to the menu name.

3 If a dialog box appears, make the selections you want. Different dialog boxes contain different elements. Following are the most common elements, as well as how to make a selection:

Tab	Press Ctrl+Tab or use the arrow keys to move to the next tab; press Ctrl+Shift+Tab to move to the previous tab.
List box	Press Alt+*the key letter* to select the list box. Use the arrow keys to select the item in the list, and then press Enter.
Option buttons	Press Alt+*the key letter* to select the option button.
Check boxes	Press Alt+*the key letter* to select the check box.
Text box	Press Alt+*the key letter* to select the text box. Type your entry.
Drop-down list box	Press Alt+*the key letter* to display the list box. Use the arrow keys to select the item you want, and then press Enter.
Command buttons	Press Enter to choose the OK button. Press Esc to choose the Cancel button. To choose any other button, press Alt+*the key letter.*

To undo a command

 Choose **E**dit **U**ndo, press Ctrl+Z, or click the Undo button on the Standard toolbar.

To repeat a command

 Choose **E**dit **R**epeat, press F4, or click the Repeat button on the Standard toolbar.

Creating Custom Menus

If you are an expert Excel user, you may want to create
macros and assign them to the Tools menu.

To assign a macro to a menu

1 Create the macro you want to assign.

2 Choose Tools Macro. The Macro dialog box appears.

3 From the Macro Name/Reference list box, choose
   the macro you want to assign.

4 Click the Options button. The Macro Options dialog
   box appears.

5 In the Assign to area, check the Menu Item on Tools
   Menu check box.

6 Click the text box below the Menu Item on Tools
   Menu check box, and then type the name you want
   to appear on the menu.

> **Tip**
>
> To assign a shortcut key, check the Short-
> cut Key check box, and then enter the key
> you want in the Ctrl+ text box.

7 If you want a description to appear in the status bar
   when the command is selected, type the description
   in the Status Bar Text text box.

8 Choose OK to return to the Macro dialog box.

9 Choose Close.

See also *Macros and Custom Controls*.

Moving Elements

When the data you are entering isn't in the right spot,
you can move it. You can move data in the worksheet or
to another worksheet. You also can move objects such
as pictures or charts.

┌ **Note** ─────────────────────────────

When you move data, all relative formulas adjust to reflect the move. Absolute references remain the same.

└──────────────────────────────────────

Data

You can choose to move a selected range by dragging and dropping or by using the menu commands. If you want to move data from one sheet to another, you must use the commands.

To move data by dragging and dropping

1 Highlight the cell or range you want to move.

2 Position the mouse pointer over the border of the selection. The pointer changes to an arrow when over a border.

3 Drag the pointer and the gray outline of your selection to its new location.

4 Release the mouse button.

┌ **Note** ─────────────────────────────

If drag and drop doesn't work, make sure that the feature is turned on. To turn on drag and drop, choose **T**ools **O**ptions to display the Options dialog box. Click the Edit tab; and then click the Allow Cell **D**rag and Drop option so that an X appears in the check box. Choose OK or press Enter.

└──────────────────────────────────────

To move data with the Cut and Paste commands

1 Highlight the cell or range you want to move.

2 Choose **E**dit **C**ut.

┌ **Shortcut** ─────────────────────────

 Press Ctrl+X or click the Cut button on the Standard toolbar.

└──────────────────────────────────────

3 Select the cell at the upper left corner of where you want to place the pasted cells.

4 Choose **Edit Paste**. The cell or range is pasted in the worksheet.

┌─ **Shortcut** ──────────────────────────────────────┐

Press Ctrl+V or click the Paste button on the Standard toolbar.

└──┘

Objects

If you place an object (such as a chart or picture) on the worksheet, you can move it to a new location by dragging it. If you want to move the object to another worksheet, use the Copy and Paste commands.

To move an object by dragging

1 Click the object you want to move. Black selection handles should appear along the border of the object.

2 Drag the object to a new location, and release the mouse button.

To move an object with the Cut and Paste commands

1 Click the object you want to move.

2 Choose **Edit Cut**.

3 Click the sheet where you want to place the object.

4 Choose **Edit Paste**. The object is pasted.

Worksheets

You can rearrange the order your sheets are placed in a workbook. You also can move a worksheet to another workbook.

To move a sheet within a workbook

1 Click the sheet tab you want to move.

2 Drag the tab to the new location.

To move a sheet to another workbook

1 Click the sheet you want to move.

2 Choose **E**dit **M**ove or Copy Sheet. The Move or Copy dialog box appears.

3 Select the workbook in which you want to place the sheet by clicking the **To** Book drop-down list box.

4 Select the location where you want to place the new sheet by clicking the **B**efore Sheet list box.

5 Choose OK.

> **Tip**
>
> To create a copy of the sheet, check the **C**reate a Copy check box in the Move or Copy dialog box.

Naming Cells and Ranges

Creating range names makes it easier to create formulas, move to the selected area, or print the area. It's much easier to remember a name such as QTR1 than the cell address that refers to that range. Formulas are easier to understand when you use range names, such as (NETSALES–RETURNS).

> **Tip**
>
> If the names you want to use already exist in the worksheet as row or column headings, you can quickly and easily create the names using the **I**nsert **N**ame **C**reate command.

To define a name

1 Highlight the cell, range, or multiple ranges you want to name.

2 Choose **I**nsert **N**ame, and then choose **D**efine. The Define Name dialog box appears.

Shortcut

You also can press Ctrl+F3.

3 Type the range name in the Names in **W**orkbook text box. Excel will suggest a name. If you want to use this name, skip to the next step.

Note

Begin the range name with a letter or underscore. Don't use a range name that looks like a cell reference. You cannot include spaces. You can use any combination of upper- and lowercase. Names can be up to 255 character in length.

4 Choose OK.

To create a name from column or row headings

1 Highlight both the range you want to name and the range that includes the headings. The headings and the named range must be next to each other.

2 Choose **I**nsert **N**ame, and then choose **C**reate from the Insert Name menu. The Create Names dialog box appears.

Shortcut

You also can press Ctrl+Shift+F3.

3 Choose which row or column contains the names you want to use by checking the check box in the Create Names dialog box:

Top Row

Left Column

Bottom Row

Right Column

4 Choose OK.

To insert a name

1 If you want to insert the range in a cell, highlight that cell. If you want to insert the name in a formula or function, place the insertion point in the place in the formula or function where you want to insert the name.

2 Choose Insert Name, and then choose **P**aste from the Insert Name menu. The Paste Name dialog box appears.

3 Click the range name you want to insert.

4 Choose OK.

> **Tip**
>
> When you are creating a formula, you can select the name from the Name drop-down list box located at the left end of the formula bar.

To delete a name

1 Choose Insert Name, and then choose **D**efine from the Insert Name menu. The Define Name dialog box appears.

2 In the Names in **W**orkbook list box, click the range name you want to delete.

3 Click the **D**elete button.

4 Choose OK.

Moving Files

See *Files and File Management*

Navigating in the Worksheet

Moving around the worksheet is one of the key tasks you must learn to use Excel effectively. Excel provides several shortcuts for moving quickly to a certain cell or range.

To move from cell to cell with the mouse

Position the mouse pointer on the cell you want, and then click.

To move from cell to cell with the keyboard

Use one of the following key combinations to move from cell to cell:

Press	To move
→	Right one cell
←	Left one cell
↓	Down one cell
↑	Up one cell
Ctrl+→	To the right edge of the current region
Ctrl+←	To the left edge of the current region
Ctrl+↓	To the bottom edge of the current region
Ctrl+↑	To the top edge of the current region
Home	First cell in the row
Ctrl+Home	First cell in the worksheet
Ctrl+End	Lower right cell in the worksheet
PgDn	Down one screen

Press	To move
PgUp	Up one screen
Alt+PgDn	Right one screen
Alt+PgUp	Left one screen

To move within a selection

Using the arrow keys to move within a selection, deselects it. Instead, use one of the following key combinations to move within a selection:

Press	To move the active cell
Tab	One cell to the right
Shift+Tab	One cell to the left
Enter	Down one cell
Shift+Enter	Up one cell
Ctrl+. (period)	Next corner of the selection

To move between sheets with the mouse

Position the mouse pointer on the tab of the sheet you want, and then click.

To move between sheets with the keyboard

Press one of the following key combinations:

Press	To move
Ctrl+PgDn	Next sheet
Ctrl+PgUp	Previous sheet

To move using Goto

1 Choose **Edit** **G**o To. The Go To dialog box appears.

> **Tip**
>
> You also can press F5.

2 Type the cell reference in the **R**eference text box or click a range name in the **G**o to list box.

3 Choose OK.

To move within formulas

1 Double-click the formula to start editing.

2 Use any of the following key combinations:

Press	To move
→	One character right
←	One character left
Home	Beginning of line
End	End of line
Ctrl+→	Right one word
Ctrl+←	Left one word

> **Tip**
>
> To delete the character to the left of the insertion point, press Backspace. To delete the character to the right of the insertion point, press Delete.

Notes

If you share your worksheet with others, you might want to add a note to certain cells—perhaps to explain a formula or to indicate certain assumptions. Even if you don't share the worksheet, notes are a good reminder of how the worksheet is set up. You easily can add, edit, and display notes.

To add a note

1 Highlight the cell you want to contain the note.

2 Choose Insert Note. The Cell Note dialog box appears.

┌─ **Shortcut** ─────────────────────────────
You also can press Shift+F2.
└───

3 Enter text in the Text Note box.

4 Choose OK.

To display a note

1 Highlight the cell.

┌─ **Note** ─────────────────────────────────
A small red box at the upper right corner of a cell indicates the cell contains a note.
└───

2 Choose Insert Note or press Shift+F2. The Cell Note dialog box appears. The note appears in the Text Note box. You can display other notes for the sheet by choosing the cell reference in the Notes in Sheet list box.

3 Choose OK.

To edit a note

1 Display the note, as described in the preceding procedure.

2 Make the changes you want by clicking the Text Note box and editing the text.

3 Choose OK.

Tip

You can use **E**dit **F**ind to search through cells and find a note. You also can select all cells that contain notes with the **E**dit **G**oto **S**pecial command.

To delete a note

1 Display the Cell Note dialog box, as described previously.

2 In the Notes in **S**heet list box, click the note you want to delete.

3 Click the **D**elete button.

4 Choose OK twice, once to confirm the deletion and once to close the dialog box.

To add sound to a note

Note

To record sound messages, you need a Windows-compatible sound board installed in your computer and a microphone matched to that sound board. You also must be using Windows 3.1 or later.

---

1 Highlight the cell to which you want to add a voice message.

2 Choose **I**nsert No**t**e. The Cell Note dialog box appears.

3 Choose the **R**ecord button.

4 Record your message.

5 Choose the Stop button to stop the recording.

6 Choose OK.

> **Note**
>
> To play the message, display the note, and then click the Play button.

> **Tip**
>
> You also can import sound files by clicking the Import button, selecting a WAV file in the Import Sound dialog box, and then choosing OK.

Opening Files

See *Files and File Management*

Outlines

If your worksheet is arranged in rows or columns with summary rows or columns, you should investigate the outline feature. This feature creates an outline of your data so that you can collapse the worksheet to display summary information. You then can re-expand when needed. See also *Subtotals*. The following figure shows an example of expanded outline.

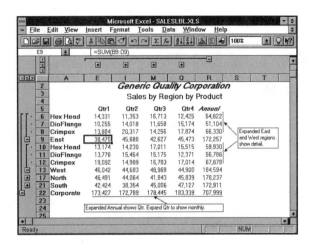

To create an outline automatically

1 Highlight the range you want to outline.

2 Choose **D**ata **G**roup and Outline, and then choose **A**uto Outline from the Data Group and Outline menu. Outline symbols appear that enable you to collapse or expand the data levels.

To create an outline manually

1 Highlight the rows or columns that contain the first set of detail information. (These rows or columns should be followed by a summary row or column.)

2 Choose **D**ata **G**roup and Outline, and then choose **G**roup from the Data Group and Outline menu.

3 Follow steps 1 through 2 for all subordinate rows or columns in the worksheet.

To display different levels in an outline

In the upper left corner of the worksheet, click the level of outline you want to display. Level 1 displays just the top or first level information. The largest number (the numbers will vary depending on the number of levels you have) displays the most detail.

Tip

You also can click the – or + buttons to collapse or expand the outline.

To clear an outline

Choose **D**ata **G**roup and Outline, and choose **C**lear Outline from the Data Group and Outline menu.

Page Setup

Page Setup options control certain aspects of your printed document—the orientation of the page, the paper size, the margins, and so on. The Page Setup dialog box includes four sheet tabs: Page, Sheet, Margins, and Header/Footer. Page and Sheet options are covered here. See *Margins* and *Headers and Footers* for information on the other options.

Note

Page Setup options are saved with the worksheet.

To change Page Setup options

1 Choose **F**ile Page Set**u**p. The Page Setup dialog box appears.

2 Click the Page tab.

3 Make any of the following changes:

- Choose either Po**r**trait or **L**andscape orientation by clicking the option button in the Orientation area.

- To scale the page, select the **A**djust to option button and enter a percentage to scale in the **A**djust to spin box. Or choose the **F**it to page option button and enter the dimensions of the pages (1 by 1, for example) in the wide and tall spin boxes.

- To change the paper size, display the Paper Size drop-down list box and then choose the size you want.

- To change the print quality, display the Print Quality drop-down list box and choose the quality you want.

- To start numbering pages with a different number, enter the number you want to use in the First Page Number text box.

4 Choose OK.

To change Sheet options

1 Choose File Page Setup. The Page Setup dialog box appears.

2 Click the Sheet tab.

3 Make any of the following changes:

- Enter the worksheet range you want to print in the Print Area text box, or click the Print Area text box and then drag through the worksheet areas you want to print.

- In the Print Titles area, click the Rows to Repeat at Top text box, and then drag across the rows you want to repeat on the top of the page. Click the Columns to Repeat at Left text box, and then drag across the columns you want to repeat at the left of the page.

- Choose the elements you want to print: Gridlines, Notes, Draft Quality, Black and White, Row and Column Headings.

- Choose the page order you want: Down, then Across or Across, then Down.

4 Choose OK.

See also *Headers and Footers* and *Margins*.

Passwords

See *Protecting Files*

Percentages

If the numbers in your worksheet represent percentages, you can format them to indicate this. You can choose from several different percentage formats.

To format a number as a percentage

1 Highlight the range you want to format.

2 Choose Format Cells. The Format Cells dialog box appears.

> ┌─ **Shortcut** ──────────────────────────
> You also can press Ctrl+1.

3 Click the Number tab.

4 Select Percentage in the Category list box.

5 Choose the format you want in the Format Codes list box, or enter a new format in the Code text box.

6 Choose OK.

> ┌─ **Tip** ──────────────────────────
> If you want a percentage with 0 decimal places, you can select the range and click the Percent Style button on the Formatting toolbar.

Pictures

Pictures are a great way to enhance a worksheet. You can insert pictures you have created with Paintbrush (a Windows paint program). You also can insert clipart files. Many applications, such as Word for Windows, provide several clipart images.

If your drawing capabilities are limited and you want to use outside artwork in your Excel documents, you can always import the art into Excel. Excel will read and translate many different graphics files so you can use them in your worksheets. You also can insert any object into Excel from an OLE compliant application and maintain hot links to the original application.

To insert a picture

1 Choose **I**nsert **P**icture. The Picture dialog box appears.

2 If necessary, in the **D**irectories list box, change to the directory that contains the picture you want to insert.

3 In the File **N**ame list box, double-click the file name. Or click the file name and choose OK. The picture is inserted.

To insert an OLE object into Excel

1 Choose **I**nsert **O**bject. The Object dialog box appears.

2 Click the Create New tab.

3 From the **O**bject Type list box, choose the type of object you want to insert into the worksheet, and then choose OK.

4 Create the object inside the program you selected, and then use the program's OK or Update command to add the object to the Excel worksheet.

5 Double-click the object at any time to return to the originating program from within Excel.

To move a picture

1 Click the picture to select it. Black selection handles appear along the borders of the picture.

2 Drag the picture to a new location.

To resize a picture

1 Click the picture to select it. Black selection handles appear along the borders of the picture.

2 Click one of the black selection handles, and then drag the arrow to resize the picture.

To format a picture

1 Double-click the picture. The Format Object dialog box appears.

2 To change the pattern or border used, click the Patterns tab. Then choose the Custom option button and choose the **S**tyle, **C**olor, and **W**eight of the frame border. If you want a drop shadow, check the Sha**d**ow check box. If you want a different pattern, select it from the **P**attern drop-down palette.

3 To lock the object, click the Protection tab. Then make sure the **L**ocked check box is checked. (You also need to turn on worksheet protection. See *Protecting Files*.)

4 To control how the object is moved, click the Properties tab. Then choose one of the options buttons in the Object Positioning area: Move and **S**ize with Cells, **M**ove but Don't Size with Cells, or **D**on't Move or Size with Cells. If you want to print the object, be sure the **P**rint Object check box is checked.

5 Choose OK.

To delete a picture

1 Click the picture to select it.

2 Press Delete.

Pivot Tables

Pivot tables, new with Excel Version 5 for Windows, enable you to summarize, analyze, and manipulate data in lists and tables. Pivot tables offer more flexible and intuitive analysis of data than the Crosstab Wizard feature in Excel 4, which they replace.

Although the data that appears in pivot tables looks like any other worksheet data, you cannot directly enter or change the data in the data area of a pivot table. The pivot table itself is linked to the source data, and what you see in the cells of the table are read-only amounts. You can, however, change the formatting and choose from a variety of computation options.

You can create a pivot table from several sources. The default (and most common) choice is to create a pivot table from an Excel list or database. In addition, you can create the pivot table from data in external data source, multiple consolidation ranges, or another pivot table.

To create a pivot table from an Excel list or database

1 Position the cell pointer anywhere within the list or database you want to rearrange. The following figure shows a list before creating a pivot table.

	A	B	C	D	E
1	Date	Staff	Project	Work Code	Hours
2	1/26/94	Merrill	USTran	3	8.0
3	1/26/94	Clayton	ZCorp	5	8.0
4	1/26/94	Garvey	ZCorp	3	8.0
5	1/26/94	Spencer	ZCorp	4	5.0
6	1/26/94	Spencer	ZCorp	3	3.0
7	1/27/94	Clayton	Selmer	4	4.0
8	1/27/94	Clayton	GP	4	4.0
9	1/27/94	Merrill	ZCorp	7	8.0
10	1/27/94	Garvey	ZCorp	4	6.0
11	1/27/94	Spencer	ZCorp	3	4.2
12	1/27/94	Spencer	ZCorp	4	3.8
13	1/28/94	Clayton	GP	4	8.0
14	1/28/94	Spencer	GP	1	3.2
15	1/28/94	Merrill	Selmer	5	8.0
16	1/28/94	Garvey	ZCorp	5	8.0
17	1/28/94	Spencer	ZCorp	1	5.5
18	1/29/94	Garvey	USTran	4	8.0
19	1/29/94	Clayton	GP	4	8.0
20	1/29/94	Merrill	Selmer	5	6.0

2 Choose **D**ata **P**ivotTable. The PivotTable Wizard - Step 1 of 4 dialog box appears. From this point, until the pivot table appears in the worksheet, you are working in the PivotTable Wizard. The buttons on the bottom of the dialog box enable you to move forward or backward, cancel, or finish the PivotTable Wizard procedure.

3 In the Create PivotTable from Data in: area, specify the source of the tabular data. Choose **M**icrosoft Excel List or Database (if it is not already selected), and then choose Next>.

4 In the PivotTable Wizard - Step 2 of 4 dialog box, define the data range you want to change. If the range is incorrect in the **R**ange text box, select the box and type the correct range, or drag on the range in the worksheet. Choose Next>.

5 In the PivotTable Wizard - Step 3 of 4 dialog box, define the column and row layout. The following figure shows this dialog box.

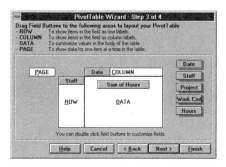

The fields are listed as buttons to the right in the dialog box. These currently are the column fields. Determine which fields contain the data you want to summarize and then drag the corresponding buttons into the **D**ATA area.

6 To arrange items in a field in columns with the labels across the top, drag the button for that field to the **C**OLUMN area.

7 To arrange items in a field of rows with labels along the side, drag the button for that field to the **R**OW area.

8 Choose Next>.

9 In the PivotTable Wizard - Step 4 of 4 dialog box, specify where you want the pivot table. Enter the upper left cell of the table in the PivotTable **S**tarting Cell (or click the cell).

10 Choose **F**inish. The following figure displays the pivot table resulting from the specifications in the preceding figure.

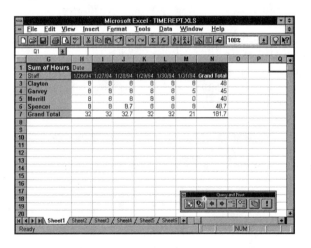

Note

After you create a pivot table, the Query and Pivot toolbar appears in the document. (If you displayed and removed the toolbar previously, however, Excel will not display it automatically.)

Editing Pivot Table Fields and Items

Because pivot tables are devices for displaying information, you cannot manually change information in the body of the table. You can, however, change the names of the pivot table fields and items. Excel does not allow you to duplicate names. If you enter an existing field or item name inadvertently, Excel will rearrange the pivot table, moving the item with that name to the location in which you typed the name.

To edit a pivot table field or item

1 From within the pivot table, highlight the field or item you want to change.

2 Type the new name and press Enter.

Note

Changing field or item names in a pivot table does not change the names in the source list or database.

Updating a Pivot Table

The pivot table display does not change automatically when you change the data in the source list or table. You can, however, update or refresh the pivot table for the following types of changes to the source data:

• Changes to data in a data field

• New or changed items

• Insertions or deletions of fields or items

To update a pivot table

Highlight any cell within the pivot table and click the Refresh Data button on the Query and Pivot toolbar.

Print Setup

[handwritten margin note:] Hide B, C Format Col Hid then select cells either side Format Col Unhid

See *Page Setup* or *Printing*

Printing

The results of all your worksheet entering and formatting probably is a document you want to print and possibly copy to give to others. Excel offers many printing features. You can choose how many copies are printed, the direction the worksheet prints on the page, whether row and column headings are printed, and other options.

To select a printer

1 Choose **File** **Print**. The Print dialog box appears.

> **Shortcut**
>
> You also can press Ctrl+P.

2 Click the **Pr**inter Setup button. The Printer Setup dialog box appears.

3 Choose the printer you want to use from the **Printer** list box.

4 Choose OK, and then choose OK in the Print dialog box.

To change printer settings

1 Choose **File** Page Set**up**. The Page Setup dialog box appears.

2 Click the **O**ptions button to display the Setup dialog box for the selected printer.

3 Make changes to any of the options. The options will vary depending on what type of printer you have. Common options include Paper Size, Paper **S**ource, Orientation, **C**opies, and Graphics Resolution.

4 Choose OK.

To set the print area

1 Choose **F**ile Page Set**u**p. The Page Setup dialog box appears.

2 Click the Sheet tab.

3 Enter the print area in the Print **A**rea text box or select the worksheet range by clicking the Print Area text box, and then dragging through the worksheet areas you want to print.

4 Choose OK.

> ## Note
>
> To print the entire worksheet, you do not need to set the print area. Excel enables you to specify what to print in the Print dialog box.

To print

1 Choose **F**ile **P**rint. The Print dialog box appears.

> ## Shortcut
>
> Press Ctrl+P or click the Print button on the Standard toolbar. You also can choose the Print button in Print Preview and in the Page Setup dialog box.

2 In the Print What area, select what you want to print: Selectio**n**, Selecte**d** Sheet(s), **E**ntire Worksheet.

3 In the **C**opies spin box, click the arrows to specify the number of copies you want to print.

4 In the Page Range area, select whether you want to print **A**ll pages or a range. To specify a range, enter the starting and ending page numbers in the **F**rom and **T**o spin boxes.

5 Choose OK.

To print column or row titles on every page

1 Choose File Page Setup. The Page Setup dialog box appears.

2 Click the Sheet tab.

3 Click the Rows to Repeat at Top text box, and then highlight the rows you want to repeat by dragging across the rows in the worksheet.

4 Click the Columns to Repeat at Left text box, and then highlight the columns you want to repeat by dragging on the columns in the worksheet.

5 Choose OK.

To set margins

1 Choose File Page Setup. The Page Setup dialog box appears.

2 Click the Margins tab.

3 Click in the margin text box you want to change: Top, Bottom, Left, Right.

4 Click the spin box arrows to set the margins.

5 Choose OK.

To insert a page break

1 Select the cell where you want the page break to appear. The selected cell becomes the upper left corner of a new page.

2 Choose Insert Page Break.

To remove a page break

1 Highlight the cell immediately below the page break.

2 Choose Insert Remove Page Break.

To print sideways

1 Choose File Page Setup. The Page Setup dialog box appears.

2 Click the Page tab.

3 In the Orientation area, click the **L**andscape option button.

4 Choose OK.

To preview a worksheet

1 Choose **F**ile Print Preview to display the preview window for the sheet.

2 When you finish previewing, click the **C**lose button.

Tip

To print the worksheet, click the Print button.

To change the margins, click the **M**argins button, and then drag the margin guideline you want to change to a new location.

To zoom the worksheet, move the magnifying pointer over the area you want to zoom, and then click the mouse button.

To print multiple worksheets

1 Choose **F**ile **F**ind File. The Find File dialog box appears. Choose the **S**earch button to display the Search dialog box.

2 Enter the search criteria to display the files you want. (See *Files and File Management*, earlier in this book.) Click OK to return to the Find File dialog box.

3 In the Listed Files list box, click the first file you want to print.

4 To specify a second file to print, hold down the Ctrl key and click the mouse button. To print a group of files next to each other, hold down the Shift key and click the last file you want to select. All files in between are selected.

5 Choose the Commands button to display a command menu.

6 Choose **P**rint.

To print a report

See *Reports*

Protecting Files

If a worksheet contains cells you do not want changed, you can lock them so that they cannot be edited or deleted. You also can add a password to a sheet or workbook.

Note

For cell or object protection to be in effect, you must turn on worksheet protection.

To set cell protection

Tip

By default, cells are locked, but worksheet protection is not on. You can unlock all the cells you want to change, and then turn on worksheet protection.

1 Highlight the cells you want to protect.

2 Choose Format Cells or press Ctrl+1. The Format Cells dialog box appears.

3 Click the Protection tab.

4 Check the Locked check box.

5 Choose OK.

To turn off worksheet protection

Choose Tools Protection Unprotect Sheet.

To set worksheet protection

1 Choose Tools Protection, and then choose Protect Sheet from the Tools Protection menu. The Protect Sheet dialog box appears.

2 Select the element you want to protect by clicking the check boxes: **C**ontents, **O**bjects, **S**cenarios.

3 To assign a password to this sheet, type the password and choose OK. When prompted to confirm the password, retype it and choose OK.

> ### Note
>
> When you try to edit locked cells, an alert box appears that tells you `Locked cells cannot be changed`. Choose OK to clear the alert box.

To set workbook protection

1 Choose **T**ools **P**rotection, and then choose Protect **W**orkbook from the Tools Protection menu. The Protect Workbook dialog box appears.

2 Select the element you want to protect by clicking the **St**ructure check box or **W**indows check box.

3 To assign a password to this workbook, type the password and choose OK. When prompted to retype the password, type it again and then choose OK.

To set object protection

1 Click the object to select it.

2 Choose F**o**rmat Obj**e**ct or press Ctrl+1. The Format Object dialog box appears.

3 Click the Protection tab.

4 Check the **L**ocked check box.

5 Choose OK.

6 Turn on worksheet protection, as described earlier.

Reports

If you work with views or scenarios, consider using the Reports feature. This feature enables you to group views and scenarios into one report. You then can print the resulting report as if it were a single document.

To create a report

1 Choose File Print Report. The Print Report dialog box appears.

2 Click the Add button. The Add Report dialog box appears.

3 Type the name of the report you want to create in the Report Name text box.

4 Choose the Sheet, View, and Scenario you want by selecting them from the drop-down list boxes.

5 Choose the Add button. Repeat steps 4 through 5 to add more sections to the report. The Sections in this Report list box show the sections in the order they will appear on the report.

6 To print the report with continuous page numbers, choose the Use Continuous Page Numbers check box.

7 Choose OK to return to the Print Report dialog box.

8 Choose Close, or if you want to print now, choose Print.

To change the report order

1 Choose File Print Report. The Print Report dialog box appears.

2 Click the Edit button. The Edit Report dialog box appears.

3 In the Sections in the Report list box, click the section you want to change.

4 To delete a section, choose the Delete button. To move the selected item up or down in the list, choose the Move Up or Move Down buttons.

5 To return to the Print Report dialog box, choose OK.

6 Choose Close.

To print a report

1 Choose **F**ile Print **R**eport. The Print Report dialog box appears.

2 In the **R**eports list box, select the name of the report you want to print.

3 Choose the **P**rint button. The Print dialog box appears.

4 Enter the number of **C**opies you want to print, and then choose OK.

Rounding

Depending on the numeric format you have chosen, Excel may round the number that is displayed. (The original number still is used in calculations.) Changing the numeric format is one method for rounding numbers. You also can use the ROUND function to round a number. See *Functions*.

To round numbers using a numeric format

1 Highlight the range you want to format.

2 Choose **F**ormat **C**ells or press Ctrl+1. The Format Cells dialog box appears.

3 Click the Number tab.

4 From the **F**ormat Codes list box, select a numeric format with the decimal precision you want.

5 Choose OK.

Row Heights

Just as you can adjust column width, you can adjust the row height. You might want more room between the rows in your worksheet.

> ┌ **Note** ─────────────────────
> When you change the font, Excel automati-
> cally adjusts the row height so that the font
> fits.

To change the height of a row

1 Highlight the rows you want to change.

2 Choose Format Row, and then choose Height from
the Format Row menu. The Row Height dialog box
appears.

3 In the Row Height text box, enter the value you want
from 0 to 409, representing the row height in points.

4 Choose OK.

> ┌ **Tip** ─────────────────────
> You also can use the mouse to change the
> row height. Click the border below the row
> heading number you want to change. Drag
> the border up or down to change the row
> height.

To change a row height automatically

1 Highlight the row you want to change.

2 Choose Format Row, and then choose AutoFit from
the Format Row menu.

> ┌ **Tip** ─────────────────────
> To adjust the row height to fit the tallest
> entry, double-click the border below the
> row heading number.

Saving Files

See *Files and File Management*

Selecting

Excel is based on the principle, select and then do. You select the cells you want and then edit, format, move, copy, and so on. *Selecting*, also referred to as *highlighting*, is one of the most essential Excel skills. Excel offers many ways to select data.

Selecting Cells and Ranges

You often will need to select cells and ranges. You can select cells that are next to each other, and you can select noncontiguous ranges (ranges that aren't next to each other). You also can select an entire row, column, or worksheet with one click.

To select a cell

Click the cell you want to select.

To select a range

1 Click the first cell in the range.

2 Hold down the mouse button and drag across the cells you want to include.

To select a noncontiguous range

1 Select the first range.

2 Hold down the Ctrl key and select the next range. Do this for each range you want to select.

To select a row

Click the row heading number.

To select a column

Click the column heading letter.

To select an entire worksheet

Click the Select All button (the blank rectangle in the upper left corner of the worksheet where the row heading and column heading meet). You also can press Ctrl+A.

Selecting Objects

Objects are pictures, charts, or other objects you have added to the worksheet. When you want to move, resize, or format the object, you first select it.

To select an object

> Click to select the object. Black selection handles appear along the border of the object, indicating that it is selected.

Selecting Sheets

If you want to select a sheet, you can do so. You also can select all sheets in a worksheet.

To select a sheet

> Click the sheet tab.

To select several sheets

1 Click the first sheet tab.

2 Press and hold down the Shift key and click the next sheet tab you want to select.

To select all sheets

1 Click the right mouse button on a sheet tab to display the shortcut menu.

2 Choose Select All Sheets.

Selecting Chart Elements

A chart is made up of several elements: the axes, the legend, any titles you have added, the data series, and so on. When you want to change one of these elements, you first need to select it.

See also *Charts*.

To select a chart element

1 Double-click the chart. A gray border surrounds the chart.

2 Click the item you want to select. Selection handles appear around the item you selected.

To select special cells

If you need to select a certain type of cell, such as all cells that contain formulas or all cells with notes, you can do so with the **E**dit **G**o To command.

> **Tip**
>
> This feature is particularly useful for auditing a worksheet. See also *Auditing*.

1 Choose **E**dit **G**o To or press F5 to display the Go To dialog box.

2 Choose the **S**pecial button. The Go To Special dialog box appears.

3 Select the options you want:

Option	Action
Notes	Selects cells that contain notes.
Constants	Specifies that constants are selected (values that do not begin with an equal sign).
Formulas	Specifies that formulas with results of the type you specify are selected.
Numbers	Selects constants or formulas that result in numbers.
Text	Selects constants or formulas that result in text.
Logicals	Selects constants or formulas that result in logicals (true/false).
Errors	Selects cells that contain error values.
Blanks	Selects blank cells.

continues

continued

Option	Action
Current **R**egion	Selects the range around the active cell, bounded by blank rows/columns.
Current **A**rray	Selects the array to which the active cell belongs, if any.
Ro**w** Differences	Selects cells in the same row that have a different reference pattern.
Colu**m**n Differences	Selects cells in the same column that have a different reference pattern.
Precedents	Selects cells referenced by the active cell.
Dependents	Selects cells that refer to the active cell.
La**s**t Cell	Selects the last that contains data or formatting.
Visible Cells Only	Selects visible cells to avoid changing hidden cells.
O**b**jects	Selects all objects, buttons, and text boxes.

4 Choose OK.

Sorting

You can sort a list in a worksheet in ascending or descending order. Sorting works best on databases or lists, but also can be used for other worksheet information.

To sort a list

1 Select the list you want to sort.

2 Choose **D**ata **S**ort. The Sort dialog box appears.

3 In the **S**ort By drop-down list box, select the column by which you want to sort.

4 Select the sort order by clicking the **A**scending or **D**escending option button.

5 To sort on more than one column, select additional sort column and orders.

6 Choose OK.

Tip

 If you need to sort by just one column, you can select a cell in that column and click the Sort Ascending or Sort Descending buttons on the Standard toolbar.

Spelling Checker

You can avoid typing errors and other mistakes by checking your spelling in the worksheet. Excel compares the words in the worksheet to the words in its dictionary and then flags words that don't match. You can correct any mistakes.

To check spelling

1 Select a single cell to check the entire worksheet.

Tip

To select just a range, select the range before choosing the command. You also can highlight a word or phrase in the formula bar and then choose the command.

---

2 Choose **T**ools **S**pelling. If no misspelled words are found, the Spelling dialog box never appears. A dialog box informs you that Excel is finished spell checking.

Shortcut

Press F7 or click the Spelling button on the Standard toolbar.

3 If the Spelling dialog box appears, choose one of the following:

Change	Changes this occurrence of the word to the word that appears in the Change To text box.
Change All	Changes all occurrences of the word to the word in the Change To text box.

Tip

You can choose a different word from the Suggestions list box, and then choose Change or Change All. You also can edit the word in the Change To text box.

Ignore	Tells Excel to ignore this word and continue.
Ignore All	Tells Excel to ignore this word throughout the document.
Add	Adds word to the current custom dictionary.
Cancel	Stops the spelling check.
Suggest	Suggests some alternatives from the dictionary.

4 If Excel started in the middle of the worksheet, you may be asked whether Excel should continue checking at the beginning of the sheet. Choose Yes. When the spelling check is complete, you see an alert box. Choose OK.

Split-Screen

If you work with extremely large worksheets, you might wish you could view two parts of the worksheet at once. You can do so by splitting the screen.

To split the screen

1 Position the cursor in the row in which you want the split to occur.

2 Choose **Window Split**.

> **Tip**
>
> If you want one pane of the window to remain the same, freeze it by choosing **Window Freeze Panes**.

To unsplit the screen

Choose **Window Remove Split**.

Starting Excel

To start Excel for Windows, you first must start Microsoft Windows.

To start Excel with the mouse

1 If needed, type **win** and press Enter to start Windows.

2 Click the program group that contains Excel.

3 Double-click the Excel program icon.

To start Excel with the keyboard

1 Make certain that the window containing Excel's application icon is the active window. If that window is not active, press Ctrl+Tab until it is (or select the group window name from the Program Manager's Window menu).

2 Use the arrow keys to highlight the icon.

3 Press Enter to run Excel.

Note

You also can start Excel for Windows by choosing the **F**ile **R**un command from Program Manager. The Run dialog box appears. Type **C:\EXCEL\EXCEL.EXE** in the Command Line text box, and press Enter. (If you chose to install Excel for Windows in a different directory, substitute that directory name instead.)

Once you start Excel for Windows, the Quick Preview online tutorial may appear. Follow the instructions on-screen.

Excel for Windows displays a new workbook when it starts. A workbook is the primary document in Excel.

Styles

Styles are a set of predefined formats you can create and then apply to a cell or range. If you use bold, italic, and right aligned often, create a style that will assign these formats with a few clicks of the mouse. Styles are saved with the workbook.

To create a style

1 Highlight a cell that is formatted with the attributes you want.

2 Choose Format **S**tyle. The Style dialog box appears.

3 In the **S**tyle Name drop-down list box, type the style name.

4 To change any of the attributes, choose the **M**odify button. The Format Cells dialog box appears. Click the Number, Alignment, Font, Border, Patterns, and Protection tabs, make the changes you want, and then choose OK to return to the Style dialog box.

5 Choose OK.

> ## Tip
>
> You can add a Style list to a toolbar so that you have quick access to styles. The Style list is in the Formatting category. See *Toolbars*.

To use a style

1 Highlight the range you want to format.

2 Choose Format Style. The Format Style dialog box appears.

3 Choose the style from the Style Name drop-down list box.

4 Choose OK.

To edit a style

1 Choose the Format Style command.

2 Choose the style you want to change from the Style Name drop-down list box.

3 Click the Modify button.

4 Click the Number, Alignment, Font, Border, Patterns, and Protection tabs, make the changes you want, and then choose OK to return to the Style dialog box.

5 Choose OK. All cells formatted with this style are updated to reflect the changes you made.

To delete a style

1 Choose Format Style. The Format Style dialog box appears.

2 Choose the style you want to delete from the Style Name drop-down list box.

3 Click the Delete button. All cells formatted with this style revert to normal style.

4 Choose OK.

Subtotals

Subtotals are a quick and easy way to summarize data in a list. You don't need to create the sum formulas yourself. Excel creates the formula, inserts the subtotal and grand total rows, and outlines the data automatically. The resulting data is easy to format, chart, and print.

To create subtotals

1 Sort the data. (See *Sorting.*)

2 Choose **D**ata Su**b**totals. The Subtotal dialog box appears.

3 From the **A**t Each Change in drop-down list box, select the column by which you want to group.

4 From the **U**se Function drop-down list, select the calculation you want to perform.

5 From the **A**dd Subtotal to list box, select the column(s) you want to calculate by clicking to place an X in the corresponding check box(es).

6 To replace any existing subtotals, click the Replace **C**urrent Subtotals check box so that it contains an X.

7 To insert a page break before each group, click the **P**age Break Between Groups check box so that it contains an X.

8 By default the subtotal and grand totals appear at the end of the data group. If you prefer to show these totals before the data group, uncheck the **S**ummary Below Data check box.

9 Choose OK.

To remove subtotals

1 Choose **D**ata Su**b**totals. The Subtotal dialog box appears.

2 Click the **R**emove All button.

Summing

The most common worksheet function is the Sum function. Excel provides the AutoSum button to quickly sum a column or row of numbers.

To sum numbers automatically

1 Highlight the cell you want to contain the sum formula.

2 ∑ Click the AutoSum button on the Standard toolbar. Excel creates a sum formula and selects the range it thinks you want to sum.

3 If the selected range is OK, press Enter. Or select the range you want to sum and then press Enter.

> ┌─ **Tip** ─────────────────────────
>
> You also can select a range in which you want to enter sum formulas and click the AutoSum button to create several sum formulas at once.

To use the SUM function

1 Highlight the cell into which you want to place the formula.

2 Type =**SUM(**.

3 Highlight the range to sum.

4 Press Enter.

See also *Functions*.

Templates

A template is a workbook that has been customized to suit a particular need. You can format the workbook, add macros, insert text and graphics, and change the page layout so that the workbook includes all the key information. When you save the workbook as a template, you can create additional workbooks based on the template. These workbooks will include the same text, formatting, macros, and other elements you included when you created the template.

To create a template

1 Create the workbook you want to save as a template. You can include text, formatting, macros, and so on.

2 Choose **F**ile Save **A**s. The File Save As dialog box appears.

3 In the File **N**ame text box, type the name you want to assign the template.

4 Select Template from the Save File as **T**ype drop-down list box.

5 In the Directories list box, double-click the Excel directory, and then double-click the XLSTART directory.

6 Choose OK. Excel adds the .XLT extension to the name and saves the template in Excel's XLSTART directory.

To use a template

1 Choose **F**ile **O**pen. The Open dialog box appears.

Shortcut

 Press Ctrt+O or click the Open button on the Standard toolbar.

Note

You also can save the template in the XLSTART directory. Then Choose **F**ile **N**ew and select the template.

---

2 In the File **N**ame list box, choose the template you want. (Remember that templates use the extension .XLT.)

3 Choose OK. Excel opens a copy of the template.

> **Note**
>
> When you save the file, you will be prompted for a file name, and the file is saved as a workbook. The template remains intact on disk.

To modify a template

1 Choose **File O**pen or press Ctrl+O. The Open dialog box appears.

2 In the File **N**ame list box, choose the template you want. (Remember that templates use the extension .XLT.)

3 Hold down the Shift key and choose OK. (If you don't press the Shift key, Excel creates a new workbook based on the template.)

4 Make the changes you want.

5 Choose File **S**ave.

> **Shortcut**
>
> Press Ctrl+S or click the Save button on the Standard toolbar.

To save a file as a template

1 Choose the **F**ile Save **As** command.

2 Choose the `Template` file type from the Save File as Type drop-down list box.

3 Enter a name into the File **N**ame text box. Do not use an extension on this name.

4 Choose the directory C:\EXCEL\XLSTART using the **D**irectories list box.

5 Choose OK to save the template into the C:\EXCEL\XLSTART directory.

Text Boxes

Text boxes are useful for many worksheet tasks. You can use a text box to hold headings or titles for your worksheet reports. You can use text boxes to hold annotation information, or even create simple layouts with text boxes. If you want to add an explanation to your worksheet, create a text box. A text box can point out key information. The following sections explain how to manipulate the text inside a text box. Creating a text box is described in *Drawing*.

To create a text box

1 Click the Text Box button on the Standard toolbar.

2 Drag across the worksheet to draw the text box.

3 Type the text you want.

> ## Tip
>
> To move the text box, click the box to select it. Then touch the mouse pointer to the border until it becomes an arrow and drag the box to the new location.

To edit text in a text box

1 Click the insertion point within the text box.

2 Use any editing and formatting features you want.

3 Click outside the text box.

To delete a text box

1 Click the text box to select it.

2 Press Delete.

See also *Drawing*.

Inserting text into a text box

1 Click the text box to select it.

2 Click again inside the text box to position the cursor.

3 Begin typing.

To change text box fonts and character styles

1 Click the text box to select it.

2 Click and drag inside the text box to highlight the data you want to change. All highlighted data will change to the font and character style you choose.

3 Choose Format Object or press Ctrl+1. The Format Object dialog box appears. You also can right-click the highlighted text and choose Format Object from the shortcut menu that appears.

4 Choose the desired font, size, and character styles from the Font, Font Style, Size, Underline, and Color drop-down list boxes. Choose the special effects you want.

5 Choose OK when you are finished.

Tip

You can change the default font inside the entire text box by double-clicking the text box's border, and then in the Format Object dialog box, clicking the Font tab and making your font selections. This changes all text inside the text box—not just the selected text.

To align text inside a text box

1 Double-click the border of the text box to display the Format Object dialog box.

2 Click the Alignment tab.

3 Choose option buttons in the Horizontal and Vertical areas. Choose an option in the Orientation area.

4 Choose OK.

See also *Alignment*.

Toolbars

When you start Excel, by default, the Standard toolbar and the Formatting appear. Excel offers several
other toolbars you can display. Plus, if none of the
predefined toolbars suit your needs, you can create a
custom toolbar. You also can assign macros to a
toolbar.

To use a built-in toolbar

Click the button you want to use.

> **Tip**
>
> To find out what a button does, move the
> mouse pointer to the bottom edge of the
> button. A short name appears. You also can
> point to the button and a description will
> appear in the status bar.

The following buttons are on the Standard toolbar:

Button	Name	Description
	New Workbook	Creates a new workbook.
	Open	Displays the Open dialog box.
	Save	Saves the workbook.
	Print	Prints the workbook.
	Print Preview	Changes to print preview.
	Spelling	Starts the Speller.
	Cut	Cuts selected range to Clipboard.

Button	Name	Description
	Copy	Copies selected range to Clipboard.
	Paste	Pastes data from Clipboard.
	Format Painter	Copies formatting.
	Undo	Undoes last command.
	Repeat	Repeats last command.
	Sort Ascending	Sorts selection in ascending order.
	Sort Descending	Sorts selection in descending order.
	AutoSum	Creates a sum function.
	FunctionWizard	Starts the FunctionWizard.
	ChartWizard	Starts the ChartWizard.
	Text Box	Creates a box for entry of text.
	Drawing	Displays the Drawing toolbar.
100%	Zoom Control	Enables you to zoom the worksheet to percent you specify.
	TipWizard	Starts the TipWizard.
	Help	Enables you to get context-sensitive help.

Following are the buttons on the Formatting toolbar:

Button	Name	Description
`Arial`	Font	Enables you to select font from drop-down list.
`10`	Font Size	Enables you to select font size from drop-down list.
B	Bold	Applies bold to selected range.
I	Italic	Applies italic to selected range.
U	Underline	Underlines selected range.
≣	Align Left	Aligns selected range to the left.
≣	Center	Centers selected range.
≣	Align Right	Aligns selected range to the right
	Center Across Columns	Centers text across selected range.
$	Currency	Applies currency style to the selected range.
%	Percent	Applies percent style to the selected range.
,	Comma	Applies comma style to the selected range.

Button	Name	Description
	Increase Decimal	Increases the number of decimal points displayed in the selected range.
	Decrease Decimal	Decreases the number of decimal points displayed in the selected range.
	Borders	Enables you to select and apply borders to selected range.
	Color	Enables you to select and apply color to selected range.
	Font Color	Enables you to select and apply color to text in selected range.

To display other toolbars

1 Choose View Toolbars. The Toolbars dialog box appears.

2 Click the toolbars you want to display so that an X appears in the check box:

Standard	Includes buttons for basic Excel features.
Formatting	Includes buttons for formatting changes.
Query and Pivot	Provides useful data for pivot tables.
Chart	Displays buttons used for when creating charts.

Drawing	Displays buttons for drawing circles, ovals, rectangles, and so on.
TipWizard	Displays tips and names for elements on the worksheet
Forms	Displays buttons for creating list boxes, option buttons, and other elements.
Stop Recording	Displays the Stop Recording button which is useful when recording macros.
Visual Basic	Displays Visual Basic buttons.
Auditing	Displays buttons that are useful when auditing a worksheet.
WorkGroup	Displays workgroup buttons for attaching routing slips, sending mail, and so on.
Microsoft	Displays buttons or other Microsoft applications. Clicking the button starts the program.
Full Screen	Hides all toolbars.

3 If you want, check or uncheck any of these check boxes. (Remember when an option is checked, it is turned on. When it is blank, the option is not in effect.)

Color toolbars	Displays color on toolbar buttons.
Large Button	Displays large buttons on all toolbars.
Show ToolTips	Displays name of button when mouse pointer rests on button.

4 Choose OK.

┌─ **Tip** ─────────────────────────────┐
│ You also can click the right mouse button
│ on any toolbar and then select the toolbar
│ you want to display from the shortcut
│ menu.
└───────────────────────────────────────┘

┌─ **Note** ────────────────────────────┐
│ During some tasks, Excel turns on a toolbar
│ automatically. If you are creating a chart,
│ for example, Excel will display the Chart
│ toolbar.
└───────────────────────────────────────┘

To move a toolbar

1 Click the toolbar you want to move. Be sure to click
   the toolbar background, not the buttons.

2 Drag the toolbar to a new location.

To customize a toolbar

1 Display the toolbar you want to customize.

2 Choose View Toolbars. The Toolbars dialog box
   appears.

3 Click the Customize button. The Customize dialog
   box appears.

┌─ **Tip** ─────────────────────────────┐
│ If the Customize dialog box covers the
│ toolbar you want to customize, you can
│ move it by clicking on the title bar and drag-
│ ging the dialog box to a new location.
└───────────────────────────────────────┘

4 To add a button, choose the category you want from
   the Categories list box, and then click the button
   you want. Drag the button from the Customize dialog box to the toolbar. The following figure shows
   the Customize dialog box.

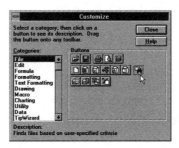

5 To delete a button, drag it off the toolbar.

6 When you are finished adding and deleting buttons, choose Close.

To reset a toolbar you have customized

1 Choose View Toolbars command. The Toolbars dialog box appears.

2 Highlight the name of the toolbar in the Toolbars list box.

3 Click the Reset button. The toolbar returns to its installed format.

4 Choose OK.

To create a custom toolbar

1 Choose View Toolbars. The Toolbars dialog box appears.

2 Type the toolbar name in the Toolbar Name text box. When you type the name, the New button becomes activated.

> **Note**
>
> You cannot rename toolbars.

3 Click the New button. A new toolbar appears on-screen.

4 Display the categories of buttons you want by choosing them from the Categories list box, and then drag the button you want to the toolbar.

5 When you finish adding buttons, click Close to close the Customize dialog box.

To delete a custom toolbar

1 Choose View Toolbars. The Toolbars dialog box appears.

2 In the Toolbars list box, click the toolbar name.

3 Click the Delete button. A dialog box appears that prompts you to confirm the deletion. Choose OK.

4 Choose OK again to close the Toolbars dialog box.

> ## Note
>
> You cannot delete the built-in toolbars.

To create custom buttons

1 Click the right mouse button on a toolbar to display the shortcut menu.

2 Choose Customize. The Customize dialog box appears.

3 Click the right mouse button on the button you want to change.

4 Choose Edit Button Image from the shortcut menu to display the Button Editor dialog box. You see a representation of the current button. Each square is called a pixel. You can change the button pixel-by-pixel to create the drawing you want.

5 To clear the existing picture, click the Clear button.

6 Click the color you want, and then click the pixel you want in that color. To erase a pixel, click the Erase check box and then click the pixel you want to erase.

7 Continue changing the color of pixels until you create the drawing you want.

8 Choose OK.

9 Choose Close to close the Customize dialog box.

Underlining

See *Formatting*

Undo

Using the Undo command on the **Edit** menu enables you to undo the last action you performed. Excel provides several Undo commands from which to choose, depending on the last action taken.

To undo an action

Before performing any other action, choose **Edit Undo**. The worksheet or chart reverts to its previous state.

┌ Shortcut ─────────────────────────────

 Press Ctrl+Z or click the Undo button on the Standard toolbar.

Worksheet Views

Excel provides many options for viewing your worksheet. You can customize the view and specify which on-screen elements are displayed. You can view a full-screen view of the worksheet or zoom the worksheet to a percentage you specify. If you need to view the same information in different ways, you can create and then change to different views.

To change the View options

1 Choose **Tools Options**. The Options dialog box appears.

2 Click the View tab.

3 In the Show area, choose what you want displayed. (Remember an X in the check box means the item will be displayed. When there isn't an X, the item is not displayed). Following are the options:

Formula Bar	Uncheck this check box to hide the formula bar.
Status Bar	Uncheck this check box to hide the status bar.
Note Indicator	Uncheck this button to hide the note indicator. The note indicator is a small red box that appears in cells with notes attached.
Info Window	Displays a window with information about the selected cell.

4 In the Object area, click an option button to choose the way in which objects appear:

Show All	Shows all objects.
Show Placeholder	Shows gray box where object appears.
Hide All	Hides all objects.

5 In the Window Options area, choose which items you want to display:

Automatic Page Breaks	Check this item if you want to see page breaks on-screen.
Formulas	Check this item if you want to see formulas (rather than results).
Gridlines	Uncheck this item if you want to hide the gridlines. If the Gridlines option is selected, you can change the color of the gridlines by clicking an option in the Color drop-down list box.

Row & Column Headers	Uncheck this option if you want to hide the row and column headings.
Outline Symbols	Uncheck this option if you want to hide outline symbols. (Outline symbols only appear when you have created an outline.)
Zero Values	Uncheck this option if you want to hide cells that contain 0.
Horizontal Scroll Bars	Uncheck this option if you want to hide the horizontal scroll bars.
Vertical Scroll Bars	Uncheck this option if you want to hide the vertical scroll bars.
Sheet Tabs	Uncheck this option if you want to hide the sheet tabs.

6 Choose OK.

To display a full-screen view

Choose View Full Screen. You see only the menu bar, worksheet, and sheet tabs. The formula bar, toolbars, and status bars are hidden; however, toolbars that were displayed in the worksheet area remain visible.

> ### Note
>
> To return to the original view, choose View Full Screen again or click the Full Screen button that appeared on-screen.

To zoom the view

1 Choose View Zoom. The Zoom dialog box appears.

2 Select the magnification you want by clicking an option button or choosing the Fit Selection option button to allow a selected range to fit in the current window. You also can enter a magnification percentage in the **C**ustom text box.

3 Choose OK.

Tip

 You also can use the Zoom Control button on the Standard toolbar. Click the button to display a drop-down list box of zoom percentages. Select the percentage you want.

To create a new view

1 Make any changes to the view you want to save.

2 Choose **V**iew **V**iew Manager. The View Manager dialog box appears.

3 Click the **A**dd button. The Add View dialog box appears.

4 Type the name of the view in the **N**ame text box.

5 Check or uncheck either of these check boxes:

Print Settings   Saves the currently selected print options.

Hidden **R**ows & Columns   Saves hidden rows and columns as part of the view.

6 Choose OK.

To select a view

1 Choose **V**iew **V**iew Manager. The View Manager dialog box appears.

2 From the **V**iews list box, choose the view you want to use.

3 Click the **S**how button.

To delete a view

1 Choose View View Manager. The View Manager dialog box appears.

2 From the Views list box, choose the view you want to delete.

3 Click the Delete button. When the confirmation box appears, choose OK

4 Choose Close to close the View Manager dialog box.

Index

GO AHEAD. PLUG YOURSELF INTO
PRENTICE HALL COMPUTER PUBLISHING.

Introducing the PHCP Forum on CompuServe®

Yes, it's true. Now, you can have CompuServe access to the same professional, friendly folks who have made computers easier for years. On the PHCP Forum, you'll find additional information on the topics covered by every PHCP imprint—including Que, Sams Publishing, New Riders Publishing, Alpha Books, Brady Books, Hayden Books, and Adobe Press. In addition, you'll be able to receive technical support and disk updates for the software produced by Que Software and Paramount Interactive, a division of the Paramount Technology Group. It's a great way to supplement the best information in the business.

WHAT CAN YOU DO ON THE PHCP FORUM?

Play an important role in the publishing process—and make our books better while you make your work easier:

- Leave messages and ask questions about PHCP books and software—you're guaranteed a response within 24 hours
- Download helpful tips and software to help you get the most out of your computer
- Contact authors of your favorite PHCP books through electronic mail
- Present your own book ideas
- Keep up to date on all the latest books available from each of PHCP's exciting imprints

JOIN NOW AND GET A FREE COMPUSERVE STARTER KIT!

To receive your free CompuServe Introductory Membership, call toll-free, **1-800-848-8199** and ask for representative **#K597**. The Starter Kit Includes:

- Personal ID number and password
- $15 credit on the system
- Subscription to CompuServe Magazine

HERE'S HOW TO PLUG INTO PHCP:

Once on the CompuServe System, type any of these phrases to access the PHCP Forum:

GO PHCP	**GO BRADY**
GO QUEBOOKS	**GO HAYDEN**
GO SAMS	**GO QUESOFT**
GO NEWRIDERS	**GO PARAMOUNTINTER**
GO ALPHA	

Once you're on the CompuServe Information Service, be sure to take advantage of all of CompuServe's resources. CompuServe is home to more than 1,700 products and services—plus it has over 1.5 million members worldwide. You'll find valuable online reference materials, travel and investor services, electronic mail, weather updates, leisure-time games and hassle-free shopping (no jam-packed parking lots or crowded stores).

Seek out the hundreds of other forums that populate CompuServe. Covering diverse topics such as pet care, rock music, cooking, and political issues, you're sure to find others with the same concerns as you—and expand your knowledge at the same time.